Music: Black, White and Blue

MUSIC: BLACK, WHITE & BLUE

A sociological survey of the use and misuse of Afro-American music

by **Ortiz Walton**

William Morrow & Company, Inc.
New York 1972

Walton, Ortiz.
    Music.

    Includes bibliographical references.
    1. Negro Music—History and criticism. I. Title.
ML3556.W248M9   781.7'73   72-7520
ISBN 0-688-00025-8
ISBN 0-688-50025-5 (pbk)

To my father, Peter

Preface

Books on Afro-American music rarely attempt to place this music within the general framework of American society and within the specific structure of the music industry. Most books on the subject are written with careful attention paid to the personalities (eccentricities) and aesthetic considerations of famous black musicians. The result is that many readers and devotees of Afro-American music are left with glamorous and superficial impressions. Stars, it seems, are born overnight, only to fade soon into obscurity. The current music suddenly and inexplicably becomes old-fashioned and new fads appear out of nowhere. Studies of this nature focus on events in the music field as either lacking causation, or as the simplistic result of glamorous personalities.

This book goes beyond that and takes into account the social and cultural matrix within which the phenomenon of Afro-American music is created, the structure of the industry dominated by ethnic groups other than Afro-Americans, and the music as a force with an existence of its own. This is not so much a history of black music as it is a sociological study of its development, its use and misuse.

To gain insight into the highly complex universe of Afro-American music, the musics of Europe and Africa and the respective value orientations they have within their cultures will be compared. (Afro-American music is conceptualized as a derivative of African music tempered by the American experience.) The effects and influences of African and Afro-American music on Euro-American society and music culture will be analyzed, as well as the converse influences, particularly in the areas of production, manufacture and distribution of Afro-American musical products.

My lack of attention to "serious" black composers is deliberate. I have conceptualized Jazz as *the American classical music*, to be differentiated from classical musics played by American symphony orchestras, which generally derive from European cultural sources, techniques and musical theories. Ideally, a volume on Afro-American music should deal with black composers such as William Grant Still, Ulysses Kay, Arthur Cunningham, Olly Wilson, Noel DaCosta, etc., and their accomplishments along with, rather than in juxtaposition to, other serious American black composers such as Scott Joplin, Edward Ellington, "Bud" Powell and Miles Davis. This is not to be construed as disrespect for the black "serious" composer but rather as the conclusion of a thoughtful sociological analysis of the American music culture as seen through un-rose-colored glasses.

Throughout the book I have put particular stress on the cultural and social underpinnings of black music which, for analytic purposes, has been divided into such categories as religious music, slave music, Blues, etc. It should be remembered that in reality black music is a unity not to be broken in time or space.

With this approach, it is hoped that the reader will be able to go beyond the superficial musical fads, and the imitations, and learn to listen to and appreciate more thoroughly black music and culture. It is a world which has little to do with the visual, but is an audio-tactile world of intense subtlety. It is also a world of sensory participation, in which the reader is invited to share— that is, if he has learned the art of listening.

The following persons lent assistance to me: my editor, Phil Petrie; my wife, Carol Walton; and artists/musicians Ishmael Reed, Romare Bearden, William Summers, Robert Feldman, Al Young, Harry Mann and Martha and William Young.

Contents

1

African and European Music

AFRICA is at once the most romantic and the most
tragic of continents. Its very names reveal its mystery
and wide-reaching influence. It is the "Ethiopa" of the
Greek, the "Kush" and "Punt" of the Egyptian, and the
Arabian "Land of the Blacks." To modern Europe it is
the "Dark Continent" and "land of Contrasts"; in literature it is the seat of the Sphinx, gnomes, and pixies, and
the refuge of the gods; in commerce it is the slave mart
and the source of ivory, ebony, rubber, gold, and dia-
monds. What other continent can rival in interest this
Ancient of Days?

There are those, nevertheless, who would write universal history and leave out Africa. . . .
                                        —W. E. B. Du Bois

The omission of Africa from world history was a problem
in Du Bois' day. Now the situation has reversed itself.
Africa is included in all books of "universal history" but
is treated as a monolith. The writers, seemingly, are igno-
rant of the fact that it is the world's second-largest continent (Asia is the first) and one of enormous diversity,
containing the world's greatest desert, largest river, in
fact every sort of physical feature, climate, plant and
animal life imaginable. There is not one Africa. Thus, in
writing of *African music*, I am writing primarily of the
music of West Africa (that area from which most American

slaves came) and even here it must be recognized that there are variations from one West African group to another. There are, however, constant features in their various musics and it is these which will concern me. For it is my belief that these constants—collective participation, improvisation, antiphony, polyphony, heightened rhythm—were passed on to, and are alive in, Afro-American music; alive, even though a deliberate plan was executed to deprive Blacks of their African culture. It is obvious to me that only easily available cultural attributes—the outward, physical manifestations of that culture and its artifacts—were amenable to destruction (specific languages, specific knowledge of tribal origins, customs, and African socio-economic organization). What persevered and developed were the *essential qualities* of the African world view, a view concerned with metaphysical rather than purely physical interrelationships such as that between music and poetry, religious function and practice, and man and nature.

Because the foregoing qualities are difficult if not impossible to circumscribe and measure, many scholars, both European and Afro-American, have denied their transmission. Undeniably, the social and economic ramifications of slavery altered the specific manifestations and functions of the African world view, producing a distinct Afro-American style and content. Nonetheless, some of its important attributes were transmitted to America and recast into forms having an independent character of their own.

Collective Participation

A characteristic of African arts in general, and music-dance in particular, is the element of *collective participation*. Without participation African cultural transmissions to America would have been seriously attenuated, for it is here that the seeds of cultural development germinate and sustain tradition. Participation in Afro-American musical performance has functioned as a "teaching tool" in place of the European-style conservatory, which has never been available to Blacks as a training center (and preservative) for their art and music. The role of the black church and its antiphonal music is noteworthy in this respect, since so many black musicians have come from its ranks. They received their early musical training as participants in, rather than passive consumers of, the musical process.

Audience involvement which is closely related to African religious rites is an artistic sharing which is not to be found in the performances of Western "classical" music. Imagine a symphony audience snapping its fingers or saying "Yeah, baby, swing." Such behavior would be quite unlikely since a symphonic concert is a one-way process, i.e., the orchestra performs *for* the audience and the only feedback permissible is applause, a quite stylized form of appreciation, *after* the performance is completed. In black music, collective participation is one of the elements to which white listeners are particularly attracted. Handclapping during performances is not only tolerated, but is taken as a sign of ardent approval. Finger popping and foot tapping are two other tactile expressions that also take place during a black music performance, in addition to various forms of verbal exclamation. These are considered vehicles of audience emotional involvement and participation which help to motivate the artist.

Language and Music

Africans' musical sensibilities are actuated and reinforced through the widespread use of their languages, which are tonal. In tonal language, the same word can have several meanings depending on the pitch of the word. Take, for instance, *fo* and *da* in the Yoruba language: *

---

* The Yoruba still live in the area from which the majority of slaves came.

Lo fò awo nyen ("Go and wash that plate") becomes, with a change of accent on *fo*,
Lo fó awo nyen: "Go and break that plate."

Olorun lo dà mi ("God made me") becomes, with a change of accent on *da*,
Olorun lo dá mi: "God betrayed me."

Many Africans are carefully educated from childhood to distinguish differences in pitch. Pitch acuity and differentials, combined with the rhythmic accents inherent in all languages, give to African languages an inherent musicality. There is a built-in musical aesthetic, such that when words are spoken for reasons of communication, a quasi-musical performance is rendered as well. In fact, one Nigerian musicologist reports that "Yoruba folksongs are, without exception, sung to the tonal inflection of words. . . . So much is this the case that when they [Yorubas] listened to simple melodies like the bugle call, the Alberti Bass, or 'La Paloma,' they readily found words to them. . . . Yoruba music is entirely governed by the tonal inflection of words." *

A heightened musical sensibility, the result of tonal language and education to pitch value, was readily transferred to instrumental music and in some cases led to "talking" instruments—drums. The dundun, the most well-known of African talking drums, is capable not only of representing the tones of the language but also the modulations. † The talking drum does not use a kind of Morse Code system (one short thump means this, one long thump means that) as imagined by most non-Africans, but is instead the immediate reproduction of speech through pitch. It is a script intelligible to every

* Ekundayo Phillips, *Yoruba Music (African)* (Johannesburg: African Music Society, 1933), p. 4.

† The West African dundun is capable of a melodic range beyond an octave, with imitations of African words made possible by alternately squeezing and relaxing the arm pressure on the leather thongs to raise or to lower the pitch. The right hand strikes the upper drum head with a beater.

trained person, only it is directed to the ear and not the eye. The young European learns in school to connect optical phonetic signs with their meanings, in the same way the young African had formerly to learn the art of understanding the acoustical phonetic signs of the drums.

Since the inculcation of Western languages and methods of education, the drum script has been all but lost. The official drummers, who once were chosen carefully for their work and were considered sacred, were discouraged from practicing their art. Even so, the basic texture, rhythms and linguistic influences were preserved in both African and Afro-American music. For this reason the drums were forbidden during the slave era (see Chapter 2).

Africans acquired at an early age the principles of music because these were an intrinsic part of their language education. Perhaps this goes a long way toward explaining the seminal influence exerted by music on Africans and also why it involves such a high degree of group participation, resulting in a collective art form.

African Instruments

Rhythm plays such an important role in African music that many assume the drums are its *only* instruments. This is not true. There is an ecological relationship between instruments and environment. In West Africa, where forests and trees abound, there are large wooden drums. In some areas of East Africa, especially in the sparsely treed highlands of Kenya, horns instead of drums are dominant. In such cases rhythmic impulses are derived from rattles or bells placed on the arms or the legs. In some cases there are no drums (see Appendix, p. 168).

Western musical instruments, on the other hand, have been diverted from nature and toward the mechanical, elaborate and expensive à la Kay, Conn or Stradivarius. The early Italian violin makers strived for purity of musical sound, deserting, to a certain extent, emphasis upon the aural-physical *experience* of music. But at base these instruments operate fundamentally on the same principle as do the African instruments; and considering the long tradition of these African instruments, they could well be the "ancestors," the archetypes of European instruments. (The Roman Empire was the final connection in a series of trade routes that extended to West Africa. Historians now know of three West African empires existing during that era, starting with the empire of Ghana in the second century A.D. and extending through the Mali and then Songhai empires, through the sixteenth century. All three empires were either near to or encompassed Timbuktu, the first stop south of the Sahara on the trade routes to West Africa from the Mediterranean or Maghreb. The city reached its zenith toward the end of this period, but all along it was a center of learning and trade, throughout Europe's Dark Ages. It is extremely plausible that African stringed instruments found their way into Italy, where in the fifteenth century the violin was "invented.")

For instance, the essential characteristics of the violin and harp can be found in the East African dom piny. (The same principle can be applied to the other members of the string family, the viols, violin, viola, cello and double bass.) Tonal differentiation is based mainly upon construction material, size and proportion, rather than upon essential structural differences.

The European piano can be conceptualized as an elaborate mechanized version of the African thumb piano, or *sansa,* made from metal strips and fastened to a hollow piece of wood or, in some cases, a gourd resonator. The strips are of graduated length (cf. graduated piano strings) so that the desired pitches, and hence scales, may be obtained. An opening is provided on the surface of the resonating chamber to enable the sound waves to escape after being amplified.

Our "Brass" family is no more than the African horns that were developed from the horns of various animals. The longer and larger the horn, the lower the pitch. A natural bell is found at the end of the horns, especially those in the antelope and elephant family, which serves to project the sound when air is blown into them. The Nigerian trumpet is an example of a horn with holes bored into it. In this manner more than one note can be played. The holes are bored in such a manner as to correspond with African scales, as was the case with the thumb piano. When no holes were bored in the horns, and only one pitch could be sounded, an African technique which they call *hocket* was employed to obtain differential pitch. Variously sized and pitched horns were played sequentially by several players, each note combining to produce melody.

As for the flute, the African form may be the prototype. Jomo Kenyatta, the African political leader and anthropologist, describes its construction:

> Generally, this article is made of bark or shrub, and it is of a *temporary* nature. A certain shrub, called mokio or mogio, is cut according to the size of flute required. The bark is slowly and carefully loosened by twisting the stem gently from one end to the other. Finally the stem is removed, leaving the hollow bark free to be used as a flute. To make the flute effective, holes are cut for producing several notes. *There is no cut and dried rule as to how a flute may be made or played.* The technique depends entirely on the individual's taste. Some people prefer four holes, others six or eight holes. The materials also differ; some people like their flutes made out of bamboo; others prefer the temporary one as mentioned above which means having a new flute almost every day. Apart from the materials described here, there is no other way of making flutes among the Gikuyu. *They do not use metal* for this purpose.*

It is important to take note of these various African instruments, because of the outstanding misconception

---

* Jomo Kenyatta, *Facing Mount Kenya* (London: Secker and Warburg, 1959), p. 93.

that all African music is dominated by the drum and therefore is solely rhythmical. Such a falsity derives from a Western bias toward melody and toward the diatonic scale—that scale so popularized in *The Sound of Music* as *do, re, mi, fa, sol, la, ti, do.*

African Scales

The scales in African music are diverse, varying in range and in number of units. In some areas they are unique to a given district or village. Hugh Tracey in his study, *Chopi Musicians,* delineates five such scales corresponding to four villages within the Zavala district of Kenya: Chisiko, Mavila, Banguza and Zandemela.* Before the Greek era Africans had developed many *scales* some of which contained the micro-tone, a much more sophisticated interval than is found in the diatonic scale, where the smallest interval is a half-tone. The intervallic ratios (scales) of the piano, which are more or less applied to other Western instruments, are fixed and standardized; *tempered.* The micro-tonic system is a non-tempered system that makes African melody more subtle than the Western ear is usually accustomed to hearing. While recording music of the Nilo-Hamitic people, Dr. A. N. Tucker remarked that his work was complicated "by the Nilotic intervals not being quite the same as those of our pentatonic." † He realized that "the scale intervals of the native's singing voice should be truer than those on the piano (which have been compromised to enable one to play in different keys)." ‡

Improvisation and Antiphony

The vocal and instrumental slurs and vibratos that have carried over into black music in America are, similarly,

* Oxford University Press, 1948, pp. 128–129.
† A. N. Tucker, *Tribal Music and Dancing in the Southern Sudan (Africa) at Social and Ceremonial Gatherings* (London: William Reeves Bookseller, Ltd., n.d.), p. 55.
‡ *Ibid.*

tones that defy Western musical analysis. In trying to
describe these tones some persons say that black musicians
"bend" the notes. The phenomenon was noted during the
era of slavery. One writer of the period said that "it is
difficult to express the entire character of these Negro
ballads by mere musical notes and signs. The odd turns
made in the throat . . . seem almost as impossible to
place on the score as the singing of birds." * These "odd
turns made in the throat" were first expressed in African
vocal music by the use of the full spectrum of expressive
modes: the glissando, vibrato, mellisma, cries, falsetto,
trills, yodels. (Those critics who hear Leon Thomas'
yodels and think only of the Grand Ole Opry are probably unaware that yodeling was long practiced in Africa
and that one of Bessie Smith's early tunes was "Yodeling
Blues.") A note given such rich tonal possibilities is capable of being shaded or molded to conform to the inten-
tion of the performer, rather than being circumscribed by
the "composer."

These vocal devices to alter the melody and to enrich
it are rudimentary forms of improvisation, and a vital
aspect of African music. Although improvisatory devices
were used in the West, particularly during the baroque
era, they were carefully measured and became fixed
by notation (e.g., explicitly noted trills). During the
baroque and early classical periods, composers and performers were synonymous, and their public performances
usually included some if not all improvisation. Composer-
performers such as Bach and Mozart often participated
in events testing improvisatory skills. It should be noted
that these "improvisors" were also vassals of a nobleman
or a rich family who paid them for their efforts. However,
the music publishing business was on the rise and sought
a direct profit from musical enterprise, especially musical
composition. Music publishing ironically freed the Western musician from the lowly position of servant that Haydn
and others had occupied, only to trap him in the tradition

* Quoted in William Francis Allen et al., *Slave Songs of the United
States* (New York: Peter Smith, 1951), p. vi.

of written composition and the wiles of commercial endeavors.

By the time of Beethoven, improvisation was considered inferior to written composition as a form of creative expression. When he came to Vienna, it was observed that Beethoven, an "eccentric young man, with no respect for polite conventions but unmistakably gifted as a pianist and improviser, . . . renounced in his written work the facile temptations of improvisation." *

Whenever a musical phrase, sung or played by a soloist, is afterwards repeated or answered by an instrumental or vocal chorus or group, antiphony takes place. It is commonly referred to as call-response or question-response form. Much of African music is of this nature, owing to the cultural demand for collective, participatory music.

> Among the Nuer and the Azande this is most prominent, both languages having their appropriate word for "song-leader," a soloist who acts as strophe, while the rest of the community replies in anti-strophe. Even when sung as solos or in unison, the songs reveal in their pattern definite traces of antiphonal origin or influence, one musical phrase echoing, or answering, or in some way completing the other. †

The audience or chorus, although being unfamiliar with the melody, could nevertheless participate. Thus repetition of phrase becomes a means whereby social participation is encouraged. In the West, the early Church discouraged this collective participation, fearing "communal singing might become too agreeable to the detriment of austerity." ‡ In fact, antiphony in the West was brought about by the Church's manipulations and regulations in getting the hymnal sung. The African soloist, unlike the Western hymnist, was in a position to vary stanza and melody, the basic ingredients of improvisation.

---

* Marc Pincherle, *An Illustrated History of Music* (New York: Reynal & Company, 1959), pp. 146, 147.
† A. N. Tucker, *op. cit.*, p. 53.
‡ Marc Pincherle, *op. cit.*, p. 10.

Instrumental antiphony was of a similar nature, with the master drummer setting the beat and patterns, followed by appropriate responses from a chorus made up of variously sized and shaped drums. It was also the role of the master drummer to lead in improvisational deviations from standard patterns. Without improvisation there cannot be freedom of artistic expression or spontaneity, both of which are essential to the West African's world view and culture.

Polyphony

Like antiphony, polyphony is widely practiced in African music and is the basis for African and subsequently Afro-American harmony. When two or more independent musical phrases are sung or played simultaneously, polyphony takes place and a form of linear harmony results. The intricacy of African polyphony is obscured by the masterful techniques and ease with which it is accomplished.

The following is an account of polyphony by an English scholar:

> The singing gave me at first the impression that the Dinka harmonise their songs. I soon discovered, however, . . . that each man, or little group of men, has his own particular song. . . . The culminative effect, especially when heard from a short distance away, is very harmonious (to European ears). Each song being in perfect time with the drums.*

Polyphony, of course, is used in European music, but its beginnings lay with the Church and its composers, which limited the music to the doctrine of the Church. It also meant that the music was very specific, beginning with two voices in parallel fifths (vox principalis/cantus firmus/tenor and a fifth lower duplum/vox organalis) and developing into a form (motet) that, in the words of

* A. N. Tucker, *op. cit.*, p. 26.

Jean de Grouchy, a fourteenth-century theoretician, "is not intended for the vulgar who do not understand its finer points. . . . It is meant for educated people and those who look for refinement in art." * (What would the leaders of Ragtime have said about that?)

Syncopation

In European music syncopation was not a natural result of its structure, as was the case in African music, but was developed as a product of the "rest." Measured music was not developed until the twelfth century. † Before that, European music was like the prose rhythm of the Psalms and other poetry in the Bible. Since most of these literary pieces are of an even, measured quality, and since the music composed during this period was often in unison, with very little harmony, it can be assumed that the music was also nonsyncopated. The music of Palestrina and Monteverdi bears this out.

In Africa, on the other hand, syncopation was a necessary and vital part of the musical structure. It was built into the music and formed part of the spoken languages which the music reflected. Little such connection between language and music existed in Europe after the abandonment of the natural scales—with the exception of the influence of the vowel-oriented Italian language. But here this influence was limited in practical application to vocal music. African languages, however, not only contained a generous portion of vowels but, as we have seen, were based upon a system of tonality and accents and formed a kind of music. But, as Ekundayo Phillips writes, "mere raising of the pitch tones could not, however, have produced speech music. At best, it could only have created variations of pure speech, much in the same manner as the tone would vary if the words were spoken by a child,

---

* Marc Pincherle, *op. cit.*, p. 20.
† C. F. Abdy Williams, *The Story of Notation* (London: The Walter Scott Publishing Company, 1903), pp. 106–111.

a man or a woman. It was the combination of raised tone
and rhythm that produced the speech music. Rhythm
was, therefore, the essence of speech music. It was there
from the beginning as much as it is present now in pure
music." * This combination of raised tone and rhythm not
only brought forth speech music but also a heightened
sense of syncopation.

Rationalization of Western Music

There is not the division of the arts in Africa that is
so characteristic of the West; art is considered no less
or more important than any other vital aspect of the
culture and is not highly specialized. (One of the rare
cases of specialization to be found in African music is in
the art of the drum, which is closely connected to religious practice. But even the master drummers played for
what was essentially a collective experience.) Every man
is considered to be an artist to the extent that every man
participates to some degree in the artistic life of the
community.

In the West the artist is apart from the group. He is
a *specialist*. It is this development that sets his music
apart from African music. Europe, unlike Africa, was and
remains a land of natural scarcity, a land of the midnight
sun, of sunless seasons, and of sons who trek elsewhere
for foods. While any explanation of it must be considered
conjecture, it is my belief that under such conditions the
culture of the people became future-oriented and moved
toward the rational and the technological. In his book
Origins of Modern Biology, Urless Lanham writes:

> The unity of man with nature was destroyed, in the
> Western world, by the technological advances made
> some ten thousand years ago when revolutionary im-
> provements in agriculture made possible the production
> of surplus wealth, the appearance of cities, and the

* Ekundayo Phillips, *op. cit.*, p. 1.

development of exploiting classes. The unity of the world view of the savage was destroyed when human unity within peoples and nations was destroyed. The chief occupation of the most energetic men became the exploitation of other human beings, while for the average man, an adaptive natural environment had disappeared, and justice had been officially postponed to the hereafter. The purpose that primitive man saw in nature was torn from its natural abode, and was now to be imposed on nature from supernatural realms. Civilized man was alienated from nature both by his mode of life . . . and by the violent distortion and dismemberment of the primitive world view into the ideologies of economic classes.*

Nature was an enemy to be conquered, rather than a godhead to be caressed. European man, having made himself external to nature, seemed forever concerned with tomorrow's plights. Permanence and predictability came to be desirables in European culture which was reflected in its concerns for the size (largeness) of things, an abhorrence of chance factors, and a virtual mania for the rational.

The process of the rationalization of Western music started with the Greek theorists. They attempted to define the magic of music, to discover its essence, by ordering music into certain modes or scales, each of which had its own *ethos* or psychological quality. And it was here that Pythagoras wed music to mathematics. This was the beginning of a system of notation in the West which has cast much of Western music into what I consider a rigid, unalterable, and fixed phenomenon.

The Church during the medieval period encouraged the invention of notational devices, but these devices were based on the Greek modes:

Let us not forget that before the introduction of *Christian Civilization* into Europe, the European peo-

* Urless Lanham, *Origins of Modern Biology* (New York: Columbia University Press, 1968), p. 16.

ples, like Asians and Africans, had each their musics and scales natural to their languages and characteristic to their races. The Europeans abandoned those ancient musics and highly interesting scales, and took as their own the *Ecclesiastical Music* which evolved from primitive Plain Chant based on Greek Modes and scales, and which the *Church* had intended solely for *Divine Worship,* and which was the music more or less natural to the *Ecclesiastical Latin.** (Author's emphasis)

One might add that this was also to a great extent an attempt to inculcate the Church doctrine contained in the chants and hymns. If only one set of notes could be selected, and if all variations were precluded, then the content could easily be controlled. Music has always been a potent social force and has occasionally been used to subvert. Ecclesiastical heretics could more easily be weeded out by their nonconformity to ecclesiastical canons. Prior to this arrangement, during the early medieval period a notational device had been worked out called *neumes,* but these only indicated the rise or fall in pitch, not the degree of rise or fall. Predictability, though on its way, was not then fully established. The final element to be controlled was pitch variation. For even though bound by the fixed notational system, the pitch of various notes was variable, and the ratios of vibrations between the notes changed from octave to octave. Bach, in *The Well-Tempered Clavier,* gave the first complete demonstration of the practical value of *equal temperament.* One octave was artificially made to resemble another. G-flat, which was formerly different in pitch from F-sharp, was now made to sound identical with it, although this process was the result of making the various intervals "out of tune." The diatonic scale took over from the nontempered Church modes and added an additional element of *rationalization* and *predictability* to the music.

European instrument makers reflected this by "tem-

* Joseph Kyagambiddwa, *African Music from the Source of the Nile* (New York: Frederick A. Praeger, 1955), p. 19.

pering" the instruments. Most of the music of the medieval period, naturally, had been vocal. The instruments that were used were either of the viol type, suited to a style of playing called continuo, or various horns that were valveless and keyless. The viols were nonfretted and resembled African string instruments. They were nontempered and could either play melody, a single note; a series of repeated notes, ostinato style; or a figured bass, which was a prearranged series of notes outlining the chords from which a written melody could be played.

Valveless horns resembling long-established African horns, as well as keyless woodwind instruments, were replaced by the highly rationalized mechanical keys and valves. These developments further show the passion for the rational and consequently predictable. Certainly the technical ability of players on the nontempered and nonmechanical instruments was considerable, since many of the concertos and sonatas written for such nontempered instruments were difficult even for the new instruments.

The order of the auditory world was finally transformed into a *visual*, mechanical, and predictive phenomenon. All a player had to do was *look* at the music, and move his finger to a certain place, and out would come the sound that had been conceived and predicted long before in somebody else's head. Instruments were now standardized, uniform, and differed only in the matter of the particular maker's expertise in their production. The standard pitch was also conceived during this process, a pitch based on an A having a vibration of 440 per second as opposed to the lower pitched and slower vibrating A of the baroque and pre-baroque periods. This gave the entire tempered scale a different timbre. The quality now became shriller, less capable of subtle variation, and lost its melancholic ethos.

The culminating achievement toward complete rationalization of music was the development of the symphony orchestra. Here specialization reached its peak, for every man had a specific sheet of music to play the same way each time. No melodic, harmonic or rhythmic deviations were to be allowed, and an assembly-line type of operation was set into motion by a foreman, the conductor. Each player, like an assembly-line worker, was expected to contribute his share to the final product. The symphony is furthermore organized along lines of maximal efficiency with a division into sections and a further hierarchy of section foreman, or leaders, and sidemen. A large clock usually adorns the rehearsal hall and orchestra members are expected to be neat and punctual. In accordance with union rules, members are given a ten-minute coffee break, where they may discuss their grievances. As in a factory there is the professional manager who collects the money and pays the workers according to their relative efficiency and position in the hierarchy. This is not the romantic conception of musicians playing their instruments in lonely churchyards in southern France, like Casals. Nor is there the freedom here that is associated with an artist like Pollack, throwing paint on walls to discover new color combinations. Instead there is the awesome impression of gravity, of men having an important mission to accomplish. Gray morning coats and knee-length tails are worn, and facial expressions, rather than reflecting the ecstasy of creation, are severe and strained. Each note is indicated not only insofar as its exact pitch, but also in terms of its loudness, intensity, duration, and even the emotional state intended by the composer. One note may thus be accompanied by four or five signs concerning how it is to be played.

As on an assembly line, if one person falls behind, or plays the wrong rhythms or notes, the whole line comes to a stop. To avoid this occurrence the foreman, or conductor, is obliged to rehearse the same music time after time, year after year. When fed up, the workers will occasionally, discreetly, sabotage the music by playing wrong notes during a concert. This throws the foreman or conductor off and he must apply all his technical know-how to return the machine to its normal functioning.

The consumer, or concertgoer, like his counterpart in the world of commerce, is a passive recipient of various sounds; that is, his reactions are private, internalized. He either accepts the product or rejects it, but he does not add his own creativity to it. Composers' names are like any other trademark signifying the quality of the merchandise. Some of these names, or trademarks, are brand names such as *Mozart* or *Haydn;* they command respect and are used in polite company. So even though a concertgoer has heard Beethoven's Fifth Symphony for the hundredth time, he still keeps listening to it, claiming that he hears something new every time. His participation is limited to applause after the finale or occasional coughing during the sections played loud enough to cover the sound. (It is highly amusing to hear the coughing of those who are not familiar with the score. They begin the tension-releasing coughing in the mezzo-forte passages, but it becomes suddenly noticeable when the music becomes softer. In such a situation the "listener" becomes embarrassed and ceases the now epidemic coughing at once, which makes it clear that the problem is not of medical origin.)

It should be apparent that this lengthy discussion of Western musical values and concepts is germane to our discussion of African music, since it is only by way of a comparative analysis that the full significance of both the European and the non-European musical systems become explicated. In Africa none of the aforementioned musical "innovations" took place and it is from Africa that the distinguishing aspect of Afro-American music emerged. The cries, falsettos, slurs and other African expressive modes found their way directly to Afro-American music during the slave era. The tendency for instruments to act as imitations of the human voice is also, I believe, a direct African transmission. Contrasted with the "music for the elite" philosophy prevalent in the West, African music retained its functional and collective characteristics in America. The mode of improvisation was developed rather than abandoned, and the rhythmic intensity of the drums was transformed into a heightened rhythmic quality in Afro-American instrumental music. Antiphony was preserved in the Afro-American church, along with the connection between the dance and music. Syncopation, vocal expressiveness, group participation and possession (the phenomenon of a church member being "taken over" by the spirits being sung to) were likewise transmitted via the church. In a very real sense Afro-American music is African music transmuted by the American experience.

2

Slave Music and the Blues

I think I hear my brother say
Call the Nations great and small
I looked on God's right hand
When the stars begin to fall
Oh what a mourning
Oh what a mourning
Oh what a mourning
When the stars begin to fall.

Africans did not, of course, abandon music and song when captured, packed into ships, and thrown into America. They continued playing their instruments although there were laws against the use of them.* In Georgia in 1775, it was decreed that "whatsoever master or overseer shall permit his slaves, at anytime hereafter, to beat drums, blow horns, or other loud instruments, shall forfeit 30 shillings sterling for every such offense." † This edict was difficult to enforce and in 1811 legislators were still saying, "It is absolutely necessary to the safety of this province that all due care be taken to restrain negroes from using or keeping drums. . . ." ‡ This was not indication of paranoia

---

* African instruments were in some cases brought over (an Ashanti drum was found in Virginia), and others, such as the banjo, were developed here.

† Herbert Aptheker, *American Negro Slave Revolts* (New York: International Publishers, 1969), p. 62.

‡ *Ibid.*

on the part of the legislature; drums played an important part in several slave revolts. A little over a century after the first Africans were sent into American slavery, a plot to revolt was uncovered in Saint John's Parish, outside of Charlestown, South Carolina. Slaves from Charlestown and the surrounding countryside assembled, under the guise of a "dancing" bout, planning to seize the armory, get arms, and take over the city. When the drums "signaled" for the "bout" to begin, the militia, hiding in ambush, attacked, killing most of the slaves. Nine years later in Stono, South Carolina, the results were different. Twenty slaves recently arrived from Angola

> broke into a warehouse and thus provided with arms, marched towards the southwest, with colors flying and *drums* beating, like a disciplined company. They had marched about 12 miles and spread desolation through all the plantations in their way. They plundered, burnt, and killed and then halted in an open field and set to dancing, singing, and beating drums, by way of triumph.*

(What were they dancing and singing? Certainly not the "Virginia Reel" and "Yankee Doodle.") It is ironic that these laws against the use of drums during the slave era, and their enforcement, account for the single most important development of Afro-American music. While retaining the essential African musical characteristics—antiphony, syncopation—Afro-American music was forced to undergo a major transformation because of the absence of the drum. Given its retention, as was the case in all other "New World" slave societies, it is likely that black music here would have sounded more like that of Trinidad, Haiti or Jamaica, all these musics having retained more of an African percussive orientation. The enforcement of anti-drum laws in the United States made it necessary to transfer the function of the drum to the feet, hands and body by way of the Spirituals dur-

* *Ibid.*

ing the slave era and by way of instrumental music after the Civil War in the new form of black music called Jazz.

Jahn Janheinz notes this absence of drums when he attempts to delineate differences between African and Afro-American religious ceremonies:

> . . . the drums are missing. *The percussion instruments are replaced by hand-clapping and foot-stamping.* No polymetry can be produced in this way and there are no specific formulas permitting the invocation of a number of Loas. The singing is therefore directed to the one Christian divinity, to whom the sermon was also addressed, and the faithful, usually many of them at the time, are "ridden" by a single divinity. The procedure which in the African orisha cult evokes ecstatic immobility, and in Haitian voodoo different types of ecstatic movement, produces in the Negro churches "Mass ecstasy." *

It seems to me that what is common among the three African peoples Janheinz mentions far exceeds the differences. A people can use only what is available. Laws were enacted in many Southern states forbidding the use of drums. Drums were never outlawed on the African continent or in Haiti. It would be a foregone conclusion that rhythmic substitutes would not have to be found in these places. Since hand-clapping is an independent act from foot-stomping, it is erroneous to conclude that *necessarily* polymetry (multirhythms) was absent. It is certainly well within the range of possibility that each rhythmic act could produce a different meter, and there are no theoretical reasons for two meters to be less polymetric than, say, three meters. In fact polymeters have always been a prominent feature of Gospel music. This is what occurs when a church audience snaps its fingers or stamps its feet in a 2/4 meter, while the pianist or organist plays in a 4/4 meter. Add to this interpolated body rhythms and what emerges is a form of polymetric rhythm.

* Jahn Janheinz, *Muntu: The New African Culture* (New York: Grove Press, 1961), p. 218.

With an Afro-American audience the hand-clapping, foot stomping and body rhythms add to the cumulative force and excitement produced by the mixture of meters propelled to a climatic intensity, unattainable with one meter. An Afro-American audience, furthermore, does not have to be told how to produce this type of polymetry. A white audience almost invariably places the first and second beats of the 2/4 meter on the first and third beats of the 4/4 meter instead of on the second and fourth. It is also why whites must usually be taught, in an explicit fashion, how to dance, their feet often colliding while moving to the first and third beats of the 4/4 measure. The explanation of this phenomenon might lie in the canons of Western theory which emphasize accents on the so-called strong beats. This rather fixed notion is connected to the rhythms of the Western military march.

> In musical parlance, [Western] meter refers to the basic . . . fixed pattern of strong and weak beats to which one responds physically in marching, dancing, or in tapping the toe. . . . The beats in a march are alternately accented and unaccented.*

Not only were the slaves forbidden the use of the drum but they were also denied the use of their language and the worship of their gods. The latter was extremely important to them. In African culture man was able to communicate directly with the gods, many of whom were very earthly and personal. They, not the individual, were responsible for the fate of the person. Monotheism was a concept which reduced the pantheon of gods to a single abstraction, the severe, constrained, highly puritanical God of the Judeo-Christian tradition. One could not get into personal communication with the Christian model of God, for "He" was too far above man, a Being you could only contemplate in the afterlife. This God also laid specific rules of behavior which went against the entire cultural ethos

* Leon Dallin, *Listener s Guide to Musical Understanding* (Dubuque: Wm. C. Brown Co., 1968), pp. 70–71.

of Africa. The body and the senses were condemned by Christianity—or at least by Christians—and the ascetic existence was considered the highest form of life. In Africa a close personal tie with certain of the more earthly gods was still possible, but now an intermediary was needed in the form of the preacher, and the rules of decorum forbade, except in a very few cases, any emotional behavior during worship. Nevertheless, the African spiritual attitude was preserved through hoodoo, the Afro-American counterpart of the West Indian voodoo. Instead of the guilt that resulted from Christianity, there was an acceptance of life and a spiritual link with nature among the devotees of hoodoo. A hoodoo ceremony was marked by states of emotional catharsis that often led to trances.

Black music here, as in Africa, played a significant role in the production of hypnotic trance states. New Orleans hoodoo ceremonies were marked by the playing of African-style drums, until the drums and finally the ceremonies were banned by public decree. Hoodoo ceremonies frequently took place in Congo Square in New Orleans, among other places. Drums were beaten at these ceremonies to help effect the trancelike state of possession. They supplied the sacred patterns and beats which, upon repetition and mounting intensity, would induce states of possession. (One can begin to see the intense psychosomatic impact of African and African-derived music.) Devices and techniques of this nature have been subsequently woven into the texture and forms of Gospel music and the Blues, and from there they have found their way into the Afro-American classical music, Jazz. In both Blues and Gospel music, repetition and mounting intensity of phrase and rhythm lead to creation and resolution of tension, punctuated by states of possession among the participants.

Those who have attended a stirring Blues performance or a Pentecostal service will appreciate the relevance of the hoodoo analogy. Common to all three is the gradual building up of tension through repetition and intensity of musical phrases leading to cathartic emotional and physical states expressed through dance, vocal and motor responses, followed by states of relaxation. The significance of music in the hoodoo or hoodoo-derived ritual is in the release of emotional tension, a health-giving property. The instruments "talk" as they invoke the Loas, the gods. The music, when possession occurs, becomes effortless, but "hot," a West African linguistic survival referring to trance.* There is an amazing similarity involving certain elements of these rites and the rites of the black Pentecostal Church.

The point is that these religious ceremonies taking place during slavery, and later within the black church, played a crucial part in preserving and passing on various elements of African music. (Heightened rhythm, antiphonal response and a collective participation come to mind immediately.) The slaves were given a modicum of freedom regarding religious practice and they used it, creating an awesome and unique body of music, the Spirituals. These "Sorrow Songs," as Du Bois called them, gave the slaves spiritual sustenance but sometimes were used in other than religious ways. Frederick Douglass, in his autobiography, cites a typical example of this secular use:

> We were at times remarkable buoyant, singing hymns, and making joyous exclamations, almost as triumphant in their tone as if we had reached a land of freedom and safety. A keen observer might have detected in our repeated singing of "O Canaan, Sweet Canaan, I am bound for the land of Canaan," something more than a hope of reaching heaven. We meant to reach the North, and the North was our Canaan.
>> "I thought I heard them say
>> There were lions in the way;
>> I don't expect to stay
>> Much longer here.
>> Run to Jesus, shun the danger.
>> I don't expect to stay
>> Much longer here,"

* Rudi Blesh, *Shining Trumpets* (New York: Alfred Knopf, 1958), p. 43.

was a favorite air, and had a double meaning. On the lips of some it meant the expectation of a speedy summons to a world of spirits; but on the lips of our company it simply meant a speedy pilgrimage to a free State, and deliverance from all the evils and dangers of slavery.*

Harriet Tubman, another African born into slavery, had a $10,000 reward offered for her return when she escaped. She had helped over three hundred Blacks escape from slavery. In a reference to the underground railroad, Harriet Tubman expressed her remarkable achievements in the face of overwhelming odds: "I never ran my train off the track and I never lost a passenger." On one occasion, when she wanted to tell a friend of her plans to run away, she sang a song containing coded words, the owner being within earshot:

> I'll meet you in the morning.
> Safe in the *promised land;*
> On the other *side of Jordan*
> I'm bound for the promised land. †

The owner was suspicious, looking at her as if there might be more in this than met the ear. Harriet was planning to return and lead her relatives up to a free state. In order to alert them for the trip she sent a letter to a free Black who lived nearby: "Read my letter to the old folks and give them my love. Tell my brothers to be always watching unto prayer *and when the good old ship of Zion comes along, to be ready to step aboard.*" ‡

As time progressed, it became more difficult to fool the slavemaster. New code words had to be found and disseminated to the slave population. Eventually repressive measures were taken. There was a suppression of certain songs, those containing any reference, however remote,

* Frederick Douglass, *The Life and Times of Frederick Douglass* (New York: Pathway, 1941), p. 178.

† Ann Petry, *Harriett Tubman, Conductor on the Underground Railroad* (New York: Thomas Y. Crowell Co., 1955), p. 95.

‡ *Ibid.*, p. 150.

to escape, and those dealing with opposition to slavery. An ex-slave recounts:

> Sometimes the masters would let us have evenings in the church. We'd sit in front with the patrolers behind us. The colored preachers would tell us to obey our masters. That's all they knew how to say. If they said something else, the patrolers might stop them. One time we were singing: *Ride on, king Jesus, no man can hinder thee,* when the patrolers told us to stop or they would show whether we could be hindered or not.*

At the start of the Civil War, slaves were put in jail in Georgetown, South Carolina, for singing the following hymn:

> We'll soon be free.
> The Lord will call us home,
> We'll fight for liberty,
> When the Lord will call us home.

Some of the slave music was sung only among slaves, these songs being uncoded. These, of course, were dangerous songs since they revealed the unmasked side of the slave, the true feelings, openly expressed. Such a song is:

> No more auction block for me,
> No more, no more,
> No more auction block for me
> Many thousands gone.
> No more driver's lash for me.
> No more peck of corn for me.
> No more pint of salt for me.

This duality of masked and unmasked music is quite significant since it is symptomatic of the origin of the dual facets of Afro-American culture. One facet is concerned with the expression of meanings that are palatable to encounters involving secondary relationships with whites, and another set of meanings is reserved for primary rela-

---

* *The Unwritten History of Slavery* (Nashville: Fisk University; *on microfilm:* Harbor Side, Maine: Social Science Institute, n.d.).

tionships involving other Afro-Americans. This cultural phenomenon continues today, especially in the argot of black musicians. It is a language in continual process of modification, since its in-group function is continuously being challenged. The musicians are literally improvising with words, something their slave forebears did quite well.

The typical slave quarters consisted of a row of cabins arranged in such a fashion that life on an individual basis was impossible. Singing, like other forms of activity, was done on a group basis. Most of the songs, as we have seen, were necessarily of an apparent religious nature and, in order to insure disguise of their true motives, were coded. The themes also reflected a communal life-style, rarely at all being concerned with the passage of one's individual life. It was as if slave music of the apparently religious type glossed over details of the personal life of the slave in favor of expressing the common desire for freedom and human dignity.

The Blues also represents collective yearnings and feelings, but here the personal life of the artist becomes the prototype of the collective. Thus one of the principal features of African music, collective representation, was preserved while the form and apparent content changed.*

Muleskinners or teamsters on the slave plantations had to traverse the area of the master's property including its perimeter, unlike the average field slave who was physically confined to one area. In order to let the overseer know where he was, the teamster would sing or holler, his voice carrying from plantation to plantation. Messages were carried this way and no doubt facilitated escape and cultural communication between various groups of slaves. This process had also important implications for black music and especially Blues. The African expressive vocal

* The form of the Spiritual generally consisted of four-line stanzas as opposed to the three-line stanzas in Blues. The antiphonal element (chorus) often contained in Spirituals was transferred in the Blues to question-answer patterns between voice and instrument.

techniques such as falsetto, slurs and trills were employed
in Hollers, with each teamster developing and initiating
his own particular melodies, style, methods of phrasing
and emoting. In this manner each singer could be identified by his own sound. Frederick Douglass, commenting
on this practice, wrote:

> The teamsters would make the wood reverberate with
> their notes. These were not always merry. In these
> bursts of *rapturous feelings*, there was even a *tinge of
> deep melancholy.** (Author's emphasis)

Douglass has captured the essence of the Blues in his
account, for he has circumscribed the seemingly contradictory elements of rapture and melancholy. This interpretation argues against the view, held by most Western
critics of black music, that the Blues is an exclusively sad
music. Nothing could be further from the truth. It is a
music of this earth and of all its paradoxes, where both
its joys and pains are synthesized and resolved into an
emotional-spiritual unity that helps make possible life's
continuance.

Hollers were sung unaccompanied, instruments for the
most part not being available to slaves. Form, as with all
African-derived music, was a function of content rather
than the reverse Western model. For this reason formal
elements did not get set in Blues until the beginning of
the twentieth century with the advent of purely instrumental Blues and the vocal Blues ensemble of the urban
areas to which black migrants were attracted. With more
than one player, some general prearranged format had
to be devised, and thus we have the beginning of the
standard A-A-B form. Field Hollers were, like the rural
Blues that followed, of diverse form, some being a single
line repeated several times—A-A; or one line followed
or answered by a second line—A-B; and at other times
a single line repeated three times—A-A-A, a form which
is most similar to the now "standard" twelve-bar A-A-B

* Frederick Douglass, *op. cit.*, p. 81.

form. The outstanding difference between the teamster who sang Field Hollers and his successor, the rural Blues artist, is that the latter usually accompanied himself on an instrument, most often a guitar. Many rural Blues artists today employ African vocal techniques as their teamster forerunners did and employ a diversity of forms, some of which contain thirteen, others fifteen or more bars, with no set metric pattern; i.e., bars may contain other than the customary four beats, with some measures 4/4, others 5/4 or 6/4, etc. The following are examples of the lyric content of some representative Field Hollers which have survived to the present:

The Wild Ox Moan
Oh - - - - - - - - - - Well, I'm going out to Texas
Oh - - - - - - - - - - to hear that wild ox moan.

Levee Camp Hollers
Boys, if you want to go down to Mr. Charlie's
and don't get hurt.
Go down Monday morning when the boys at work.

To illustrate the difference between the standardized form of the Blues and its antecedent, the Holler, the following song can be compared to the Holler above as to lyric and formal elements:

Levee Camp Blues
Captain, Captain, you'd better count your men,
Captain, Captain, you'd better count your men,
Some gone to the bushes, and some gone in.

Carrying forth the African tradition of improvisation, the Field Hollers provided a fertile ground for Blues improvisation. Alain Locke, in comparing the Work Song, another mode of slave music, to the Blues, comments:

> The work song is composed of several short lines repeated with pauses intervening for the stroke of a pick or hammer, and is usually sung by a group. The Blues form—3 line verse with repetition of final line followed

by a climactic third line—give it the proverbial twist or epigram.*

Perhaps it is because these songs were created out of a slave's work experience that they are seen as "sad songs" and have traditionally been described solely in terms of pathos. This has occurred for several reasons, among them a failure to include and conceptualize purely instrumental forms of Blues in traditional analyses, and a much too literal interpretation of the poetry or lyrics of vocal Blues.

The customary indicators of mood (happy and sad)— in terms of audience perception of purely instrumental composition and performance—are tempo and tonality. Slow versus fast tempi are generally associated with sad and happy moods respectively, while medium tempi are perceived as lying midway between the two polar opposites. The same type of association is connected with major versus minor tonality. Conceptual difficulties that surround the notion of Blues as *necessarily being sad music* begin as we attempt to classify according to mood such compositions as "Now Is the Time" by Charlie Parker or the up-tempo boogie-woogie compositions of the late Thirties and early Forties. "Now Is the Time" is written in a major tonality, and was played by Parker at a medium-to-quick tempo. Many of the boogie-woogie compositions were similarly composed and performed in terms of tonality and tempi. Of course the above examples do not represent the totality of instrumental Blues, nor even a representative sample. However, they do not by any means belong to a rare form either, and therefore require an explanation consistent with other Blues genre. What seems to be called for is an interpretation of Blues moods that allows for such variation and which in turn allows us to further refine our general conceptualization of the form. It seems to me that such an explanation requires our taking an intermediate position which interprets Blues as

* Alain Locke, *The Negro and His Music* (New York: Arno Press, 1969), pp. 28–35.

being neither wholly melancholy nor wholly joyous but rather, in most instances, a combination of polar opposites which results in a tension of mood. Juxtaposition of major upon minor tonality resulting in the production of what has become known as "blue notes" is a musicological correlate of the psychological and physiological tensions discussed previously.

Similar phenomena are evidenced in vocal Blues, if the persistence and tenacity of Afro-American culture, especially regarding language, are taken into account. The fundamental conditions prescribing the usage of sub-rosa communication between the races have not significantly altered. Language characterized by double-entendre has held persistently throughout Afro-American history, finding its way from slave music and language to the Blues lyric and vernacular speech modes of contemporary Afro-American culture. When double-entendre and secret meaning are taken into account, new light is cast upon affective interpretations of the Blues, as well as upon their sociological significance.

From the inception of Jazz, the Blues have been part of its repertoire. They have involved a wide range of tempi, tonality, timbre and mood. As in rural Blues, there is great flexibility and no strict adherence to the twelve-bar classic form.

There is a great danger in assigning the Blues to set categories, e.g., Blues as either a strictly sociological phenomenon or Blues as strictly an African music. Both views are incorrect from empirical evidence and both lead to dubious conclusions as to the ultimate forte of Blues. Charles Keil projects the sociological thesis that Blues will endure, but his reasons for thinking so are all negative, having to do with the notion of innate conflict between the sexes:

> Those who suspect that the driving force behind the blues will disappear in the harmonious and fully integrated society that the Reverend King envisions are probably mistaken, because it is conflict of the sexes

more than conflict between cultures that motivates the
blues artist to bring his troubles before a sympathetic
audience. . . . Whatever the future holds, I suspect
that men and women will have little trouble in finding
excuses to fuss and fight. These basic conditions of fric-
tion are enough to ensure the continued existence of the
blues for many generations to come, if only because no
form of music yet evolved has been able to express so
simply and directly the frustrations, satisfactions, and
reversals of the mating game.*

This argument does not, however, account for the large
repertoire of both vocal and nonvocal Blues, which contain no associations in lyrics, title or manner of performance with strife between the sexes.

Frantz Fanon argued also for a strictly sociological interpretation of Blues:

Thus the Blues—the Black slave lament—was offered up
for the admiration of the oppressors. This modicum of
stylized oppression is the exploiter's and the racist's
rightful due. *Without oppression and without racism
you have no blues.* The end of racism would sound the
knell of great Negro music. †

Implicit in this argument is the assumption that culture,
or particularly, the expressive aspect of culture, is deter-
mined only by social-political forces, to the exclusion of
other possible variables, e.g., climate and geography. But
the most serious assumption is the denial of what is readily
given for other groups—a sense of cultural heritage. Irish
living in America are accorded a sense of cultural descendancy, and so are Italians, Poles and Mexicans. Africans living in Brazil, Trinidad and Haiti are also accorded
this sense of cultural descendancy, but the black man in
America, unlike other ethnic groups in the new world, is
conceived of as having no cultural roots anywhere except

* Charles Keil, *Urban Blues* (Chicago: University of Chicago Press,
1966), p. 99.
† Frantz Fanon, *Toward the African Revolution* (New York: Grove
Press, 1967), p. 37.

in America. The problem cannot be simply reduced to one of social oppression, inasmuch as poor whites, who have had an equally long history of poverty, and now make up the majority of welfare recipients, did not create the Blues, Jazz or Spirituals. Although the social conditions peculiar to America have obviously been an economic disadvantage to Blacks, they have coalesced with African retentions to produce a new and highly influential culture and world view. The Blues cannot be reduced to a reaction against what white people do and have done; rather they would be more accurately conceived of as a positive form that affirms and preserves Afro-American culture.

The Blues as lyric/sung poetry is a medium through which passes the essence of the life experience, both its travails and ecstasies. They are immortal, not because their lyric content sometimes reflects problems produced by a social-cultural order, out of tune with the universe, but because of the infinite poetic and musical treatment afforded by their unique problem-solving properties. The portrayal of life without facade enables an audience to identify with content and mood, on an honest, personal level, even though Blues composition is usually grounded in individual experience. When audience identification with situation, content and message occurs, a group experience is shared which is supportive to performer and audience alike.

Until the turn of the century Blues was a vast matrix encompassing Field Hollers, Shouts and Work Songs mostly sung by nonprofessionals, in the strictly commercial sense of the word. The professional arena for Blues, outside of that provided within the black community, was confined to minstrel shows and vaudeville. After the notation of the first Blues, singers like Ma Rainey, Mamie Smith and Bessie Smith abandoned the unstructured, highly variable rural Blues for the now-familiar twelve-bar forms which became known as classical Blues, a term that owes itself to a Western bias toward form. "Classical" is supposed to differentiate the former period, where the

everyday man sang and played the Blues, from what in
essence was the first wave after Stephen Foster of a white
commercial avalanche on black music.

Mamie Smith was the first singer to make a Blues recording. It was so successful that record companies sought
out a number of singers (female), hoping to get another
Mamie Smith. Some of these "finds" were Eliza Brown,
Ida Cox, Lil Green, Lucille Hegamin, Rosa Henderson,
Victoria Spivey, Ethel Waters and Edith Wilson. LeRoi
Jones has astutely pointed out that the reason black
women, rather than black men, were hired for these appearances is that America could always tolerate orgiastic
interplay between white men and black women but could
not stand white girls or women being titillated sexually
by black men.

It is because of his sexual attitude that the Western
white man has usually seen black music, especially Blues,
through blinders and has misrepresented the frank sensuality and expression of the life force as something licen-
tious. This has led to an ambivalent attitude toward
black music, an attraction for, and a threat to, what
has been forbidden in the West—sex. Again, the relationship of the sensual in black music to the wider black
culture is ignored, and the elements of collective participation and ecstasy are misrepresented. The sensual is
integrated without shame into black culture.

The white listener to black music who does not know
or, in some cases, care to know of the relationships which
place sex in a context of African and Afro-American
cultures becomes somewhat like the child who yearns to
experience what is tabooed by the culture. An indication of the severity of this Western predilection can be
found in the following passage from Hermann Hesse's
Steppenwolf:

> From a dance-hall there met me as I passed by the
> strains of lively jazz music, *hot and raw as the steam
> of raw flesh.* I stopped a moment. This kind of music,
> *much as I detested it, had always had a secret charm*

for me. It was repugnant to me, and yet ten times preferable to all the academic music of the day. For me too, *its raw and savage gaiety* reached an underworld of *instinct* and breathed a simple, honest *sensuality* . . . and this music had the merit of a great sincerity. Amiably and unblushingly negroid, it had the *mood of childlike happiness.* There was *something of the nigger in it,* something of the American, who with all his strength seems so *boyishly fresh and childlike* to us Europeans.*

Hesse's hero, Harry Haller, like most Westerners, is caught in the inexorable clash between Western civilization's highest goal, rationality, and the exotic appeal of the world of emotion and feelings. The irrational areas of man's existence are seen as forces of evil, of the devil, of wickedness, and rationality is seen as good, pure and godlike in its manifestations.

* Hermann Hesse, *Steppenwolf* (New York: Bantam, 1969), p. 43.

3

Ragtime

"A year before Brahms died," said Mr. Abell, "he asked me whether I played the banjo. 'No,' I replied. 'Why?' 'Because at Klengel's I met an American girl who played for me, on that curious instrument, a sort of music which she called Ragtime. Do you know this?'—and he hummed the well-known tune which goes to the words:
'If you refuse me,
Honey, you lose me.'
'Well,' the master continued with a faraway look in his eyes, 'I thought I would use, not the stupid tune, but the interesting rhythms of this Ragtime.'"
—Verna Arvey

The importance of Ragtime to black music, and as a theoretical system to American and European music, has been forgotten because of the greater attention given to its successor, Jazz. The publishers of "Syncopated Sandy," a Ragtime composition of 1897, observed:

The authors and publishers in presenting "Syncopated Sandy" to the public have succeeded in illustrating the *absolute theory* of the now famous Ragtime music which *originated with the Negroes* and is *characteristic of their people*. Careful attention to the accent marks will enable the performer to obtain perfect Ragtime and give the basic principles *whereby any music ever*

written can be arranged and played in *Ragtime,* the
musical rage of the century.*

Pianist-composer Scott Joplin, born in Texarkana, Texas,
in 1868, is now credited with being the originator of
Ragtime. However, Joplin stands in the same relation to
Ragtime as W. C. Handy does to Blues. Both men synthesized elements of music that had been evolving over
long periods of time, and which include African transmissions and subsequent transformations undertaken in
the new environment of America. Syncopated and lyric
elements of Ragtime can be found in the Spiritual, Field
Holler, minstrel and "coon" songs—four predominantly
vocal forms.

Research undertaken by Dr. Frederic Hall of Dillard
University indicates that the roots of Ragtime go back to
the slave era, during which time slaves who displayed a
talent for music were requisitioned to provide entertainment on plantation drawing-room pianos for dancing. The
black keys were first employed, representative of the pentatonic scale, a scale widely used in Africa. Displaced (to
European ears) accents, also characteristic of African
music, were employed, lending a feeling of syncopation.
With greater familiarity of the technical aspects of the
piano the range of tonalities increased and the full range
of the piano began to be utilized.

Ragtime syncopation was more than a device of notated
accents used artfully for effect. With Joplin, whose "Maple
Leaf Rag," published in 1899, propelled Ragtime into national prominence, the form became an explicit system of
rhythmic-lyric concepts. As a predominantly piano music,
it represents the first instrumental music of Afro-Americans in which instruments were not used merely as accompaniment. The subtle use of harmonic devices such as
sevenths and ninths, the outlining of chord structure in
the rolling bass, combined with syncopation and haunting
melodic-lyricism, all point the way to instrumental Jazz.

* Rudi Blesh, *They All Played Ragtime* (New York: Oak Publications,
1950), p. 89.

Buddy Bolden's band, the earliest known New Orleans band, was known as a Ragtime band. Many of the early New Orleans Jazz compositions were Rag pieces fitted and adapted to an instrumental ensemble. Ragtime was also noteworthy in supplying a rhythmic foundation supplanting the use of African drums, which had come into disfavor as early as the eighteenth century. African instrumental syncopation, having been a by-product of drum ensembles employing polymetry, was now established in the absence of drums. Early New Orleans ensembles such as the Buddy Bolden band did not make use of drums but were able to employ syncopation due to the already developed Ragtime system. One of the reasons Ragtime was, and continues to be, a difficult music to play, is the relative independence of musical line, which results in polyrhythms and a strong suggestion of polymeters. This nonsynchronized, out-of-phase quality lent the "raggedy" aspect from which the musical system was commercially named. It, likewise, is a quality which underlay out-of-phase rhythmic displacements resulting from the mixing of instrumental voices in New Orleans Jazz ensembles, which were in the formative years often called "spasm" bands.

Contrastingly, European musical systems for the most part had emphasized a synchronization and regularity of rhythmic and melodic elements, with placement of accents on the "strong beats" lending a martial mood.

The following are some examples of characteristic Ragtime rhythms. They are not to be considered exhaustive of syncopations found in the music, but merely as indicative of some of its basic features. Notice, for example, how the first beat, or downbeat is, unlike European music, often not stressed. Examples A, B and C are Ragtime rhythms.[*]

Examples D [†] and E [‡] are rhythms of a Field Holler and Spiritual. Note the similarities in syncopation.

[*] Scott Joplin, *School of Ragtime* (New York, 1908).
[†] W. C. Handy, "Field Hollers (Rhythms) of a Negro Plowman," *Father of the Blues* (New York: Collier, 1941), p. 143.
[‡] James Weldon Johnson (ed.), *The Book of American Negro Spirituals* (New York: Viking, 1925), p. 76.

In addition to being the first black instrumental music
in America, Ragtime was also the first program music on
a popular level in America. Programmatic music is one in
which the expressive intent of the composer is capable of
being described to the listener through suggestion of mood
and event. In order to reconstruct or reenact the expressive
content of the composer, there must be sufficient silence,
and therefore space, within the music to permit the listener

this type of communication. To this extent, Ragtime expression becomes dramatic as well as programmatic, and therefore an action music. The banjo-Ragtime rhythms of minstrel "coon" songs were employed in this respect as accompaniment to such dances as the buck and wing, and the cakewalk. Later, Ragtime served to provide aural meaning to the silent, and later Western, movies, accentuating action and suggesting mood. The same was true of the Ragtime influence on the classical overture, the European-style march, of which Sousa was the most well-known exponent, French and American "impressionist" music, early American "folk" songs and the Blues. The following titles are a few of the examples of Ragtime rhythms found in marches, overtures, French and American impressionists and the American folk songs:

"Dixie"—Dan Emmett
"Camptown Races"—Stephen Foster
"Stars and Stripes Forever"—John Philip Sousa
"Central Park at Night"—Charles Ives
"Golliwog's Cake-Walk"—Claude Debussy
"Turkey in the Straw"—authorship disputed
"La Création du Monde"—Darius Milhaud
"Ebony Concerto"—Igor Stravinsky

Fast, watered-down versions of Ragtime can often be heard in Western movies today. The scenes typically feature a man in shirtsleeves, wearing a straw hat, nonchalantly plunking out Ragtime melodies on an upright piano. They usually take place in a saloon with upstairs brothel accommodations. A wide range of activities, including gambling, drinking and solicitation of male customers, are accompanied and vitalized by Ragtime syncopations. The following is a similar description of the action functions of Ragtime in a St. Louis sporting house, The Rosebud:

> The Rosebud had a bar in the front, and this, as well as
> the wine room in the back, dispensed liquor. The wine
> room, accessible from the bar or through the side "family
> entrance," was where the sports and the girls gathered

around the piano to hear Tom Turpin's strong playing
as well as the Ragtime of many others.*

Although Americans, especially American males, have
enjoyed going where the action is, it appears that this
function of Ragtime met with a good deal of puritan hy-
pocrisy. Some of the Rags had explicit sexual titles, such
as the unpublished "She's Got a Good Pussy," and Jelly
Roll Morton's "The Naked Dance."

During the period (1893–1898) when America was suf-
fering the throes of economic depression and threatened
revolution, Ragtime served as a stimulus to hope and
optimism. Even though "Maple Leaf Rag" was not the
first published Rag (that honor going to a white musician),
it popularized the form. Scott Joplin did hypnotize the
nation as the lyrics to "Maple Leaf Rag" suggest, not
sinisterly, as a Svengali, but into a mood of optimism,
staving off the mental depression and anxiety caused by
the uncertainty of the times. He and others helped to
transform the nation's mood from one of depression to
one of gaiety. Concerning the not-so-gay aspects of the
nineties that were uplifted by Ragtime, Rudi Blesh comments:

> The land was galled and restless with riots, hunger
> marches, and threats of revolution; the people overready
> to smile again and to dance the cakewalk. It was all like
> a fresh start; no past associations, good or bad, clung to
> the new music; there was not a tear in ragtime, and
> irony, malice, bitterness, or regret hid in its laughter.†

Perhaps he exaggerates the happy aspect, for Ragtime,
with its often contrasting strains of minor and major, did
contain traces of melancholy. However, for the most part
it was a happy, effervescent music.

Scott Joplin, like so many of his successors, had a right
to be melancholy, although he contributed so much of a
positive nature to American social life. Joplin's publisher,

---

* Blesh, *op. cit.*, p. 54.
† *Ibid.*, p. 4.

John Stark, who had become wealthy from the sheet music sales of "Maple Leaf Rag," deserted him in 1909. Stark did not want to pay royalties for Joplin's subsequent pieces, insisting on outright payments, a condition favorable to the publisher in the event of a "hit." Joplin's 504 piano pieces included marches, waltzes and cakewalks, as well as conventional Rags. He wrote a ballet, and two Ragtime operas, *Guest of Honor* and *Treemonisha. Treemonisha,* after the labors of black composer, T. J. Anderson, was in 1971 given a performance in Atlanta, Georgia. Harold Schonberg of *The New York Times* noted that it was a period piece (like Puccini's *Girl of the Golden West,* I suppose) that had moments of genius and eccentricity.

Anderson's efforts on behalf of Scott Joplin are atypical ones for black musicians. With the many fine Afro-American pianists in America, it took Joshua Rivkin, a Jew, to perform the recent release of eight Joplin rags. Like the Afro-American minstrels who applied burnt cork to blacken their faces, in order to imitate the whites who were imitating them, many of today's Afro-American musicians likewise imitate their imitators. This tendency is expressed in the preference for electronic instruments and gadgetry, and a disinclination to swing or play with a pronounced beat. To this group of players both acoustic instruments and a hard-swinging beat are old fashioned.

After the incident with Stark, Joplin was beset by what some called "delusions of persecution." He felt that his music and his ideas were being stolen.

Joplin's concern with the theft of his music was, in general terms, not unfounded. Mechanical sound reproduction developed greatly during his era, and aided in the dissemination of this aspect of black culture (Ragtime) to America. This and subsequent technological developments resulted in a lack of control over the product on the part of the creators. An early model of the pianola was invented in 1825. However in 1897, two years before publication of "Maple Leaf Rag," a more efficient model was placed on the market. Heretofore, sheet music had predominated, finding its way to an increasingly larger audience after the Stark publication of "Maple Leaf" sheet music. Sheet music appealed primarily to the social-entertainment needs of the American family. The family activities coalesced around the piano, and fulfilled a function that is now performed by the television set. Even though this allowed many persons to get involved in musical production, professional musicians were not particularly threatened since the printed music alone was insufficient as a model for imitation. Before the advent of the pianola, the would-be imitator had to go directly to the source, which was, in the case of Ragtime, most often found in the black community.

Within this community, stringent efforts were made to protect techniques and original concepts that were frequently the result of years of arduous practice. Several New Orleans interviewees, survivors of the early Jazz movement, spoke of handkerchiefs being placed around trumpet valves to prevent inspection of fingering technique. Another interviewee told of clipping off the tops of the music to remove titles. Numbers were written where the titles had formerly been and were used by the leaders in calling out compositions for performance. In this manner, even the seemingly innocuous sheet music could be protected from those who sought to avoid the effort of self-discovery. This is probably why musicians speak of "playing a number" rather than referring to specific titles.

The technology of the player piano opened up a new possibility: a performance could now be repeated on a machine, sounding the same way each time, thus allowing for a more or less exact replication of note, style and mood. Professional as well as amateurs who had been unable to capture a certain style were now in a position to strengthen their playing or as one writer puts it, "develop the tradition." The place of a creator like Joplin would then be lost in the clamor of competitors once the idea or concept was given wide circulation via mechanical sound reproduction. Control over product would be further weakened since it was now possible to read as well as hear black-created music outside its place of origin Joplin recorded at least seven piano rolls, some of which were issued on more than one label.

To illustrate how, in each black music era from early slavery to the present, the music has first been keenly listened to by whites and then imitated by the animatronics (a Disneyland term for *robot*) to be fed to the white culture, making that all the richer and Afro-American artists all the poorer, let me offer you the following excerpt from The Toronto Ragtime Society publication on Scott Joplin:

> Many had tried to copy Joplin with little enough success. *Although this distinction may at first seem shadowy*, the young white man, Joseph Lamb, emulated rather than copied the master. He was able to do this because he possessed a rare ability. He could penetrate to the very sources of the developed and personal style of the other man. To his ability, he added another perhaps even rarer: that of channeling his own great creative powers into that style. . . . The musical career of Joseph Lamb conclusively points up two facts. One is that classical ragtime, *though of Negro origin*, had become with Joplin a *music for all America.** (Author's emphases)

Or would it have been more correct to say that "classical" Ragtime had become, with white Joseph Lamb, the composer of "Coontown Frolics" (1900), a music for all America?

In the fall of 1916, Scott Joplin was *removed* to the Manhattan State Hospital on Ward's Island in the East River along the strait called Hell's Gate. On April 1, 1917, Scott Joplin died. "For one day, Scott Joplin was a famous man even in Harlem. That was the day of his long and impressive funeral." †

* Paper on Scott Joplin published by Ragtime Society, Ontario, Canada.
† *Ibid.*

4

New Orleans Jazz

Sunday was your big day at the lake. Out at the lake-
front and Milneberg there'd be 30–35 or 40 bands out
there. The clubs would all have a picnic and have their
own band or hire one. All day you would eat chicken,
gumbo, red beans and rice, barbecue, and drink beer
and claret wine. The people would dance to the bands,
or listen to them, swim, go boatriding or walking on the
piers. The food was mostly every tub, that means everybody takes what he wants and waits on himself. The
musicians had just as much fun as the people you
played for.

—Pops Foster

Set amid stately palms and fragrant magnolia trees, provided with two major waterways, the Mississippi and the
Gulf of Mexico, lies the "Crescent City," New Orleans.
One cannot help being impressed by the stately mansions
with their ornate balconies of wrought-iron Spanish fili-
gree, the winding streets in the *vieux carré* section, the
uptown area which still abounds with numerous African
carryovers, and especially its good-natured hedonism and
frank bawdiness. However, beneath the surface of this
fun-loving good nature lies a peculiar tension, as though
a hidden rationale existed to justify the pleasure-seeking
of its inhabitants. These tensions become manifest when
one observes Blacks and whites living back-to-back of

each other, but rarely on the same street, a modified yet distinct form of residential segregation. Likewise, the observer hears some of the Creoles speak proudly of their long artisan tradition that in large part built the city, of their long family lineage with its inevitable French blood, and of their disdain for the "Yankees."

Among some of his uptown brothers, one may hear vituperative denouncements of "high-yaller," *passé blanc*, uppity Creoles, along with the somewhat contradictory claims of white or Creole grandmothers or cousins.*

Among whites, many of them with dark skin, blue-black hair and full lips, one can hear denouncements of "poor white trash," "niggers," and, in short, of everyone outside of Creoles (so-called white Creoles, that is).

The question soon becomes one of who is white and who is black in this city of polyglot racial and ethnic mixtures, and one is reminded of the insightful passage from the novel *Black No More*, by George Schuyler, where Dr. Buggerie, the statistician, unfolds his findings on "miscegenation" in America to Mr. Snobbcraft, the professional Anglo-Saxon. "A certain percentage of these Negroes . . . in time lightened sufficiently to be able to pass for white. They then merged with the general population. Assuming that there were one thousand such cases fifteen generations ago—and we have proof that there were more—their descendants now number close to fifty million souls." †

* The term *Creole* is fraught with ambiguity. Some contemporary Afro-American historians interpret the confusion over definition as a conscious attempt to conceal policies of racial and cultural assimilation pursued under French rule in Louisiana. *Webster's International Dictionary* lists three principal definitions of *Creole*: 1) One of native birth out of European descent; 2) A white person descended from early French or sometimes Spanish settlers of the Southern U. S. especially in the gulf states and preserving a characteristic form of French speech and culture; 3) A person of mixed French and Negro descent speaking a dialect of French or Spanish.

† Eric Lincoln reports that Robert Stuckert of Ohio State University estimates the number of white persons of Negro extraction at 28 million, or 21% of the U. S. population (based on 1960 census figures).

Of course, *Black No More* is a novel and therefore belongs more in the realm of fiction than science; however, it does present some well-formulated hypotheses, with logically drawn propositions—such as the foregoing, and thus as fiction its tenability is increased. And since color or complexion was, and still is, very much a criterion for status position, and one of the chief factors in status anxiety in New Orleans, the quotation is germane to our discussion coupled with the voodoo aesthetic. For it is my belief that it is out of this status anxiety that Jazz developed.

Discussions of New Orleans Jazz traditionally focus on aesthetic descriptions of style and content. A good deal of attention is also paid to outstanding individual performers such as Buddy Bolden or Baby Dodds. What has been missing in the research and literature on Jazz is a systematic analysis and placement of New Orleans Jazz, its performance and its performers, within the context of the city's *social structure*.

Cross-cultural analyses of musical form, style and content suggest that the functional requirements of a particular music differ according to social structure. Thus in African society, characterized by communalism, an emphasis is placed on collective musical expression, often in the form of antiphony. Rhythmic acuity in African music is reinforced by the requirements of the ceremonial dance and results in a wide usage of the drums and other percussive instruments. By way of contrast, the elitist social structure of sixteenth- and seventeenth-century Europe responded to the rococo chamber music style, functional for a small listening audience rather than for dancing. Its nonsyncopated polyphony and the use of soft, quiet, stringed viols were suitable to performances in small rooms (chambers) for elite patrons of the arts.

The implications of varying social systems for the development of musical style are of course more complex than the above examples suggest. Their inclusion here is due to a desire to clarify and indicate the nature of the research problem.

Certainly New Orleans Jazz was not the only, or even the first, major form of American music. As we have seen, Spirituals, Field Hollers, Blues and Ragtime had preceded it. But there were significant differences in style, thematic emphasis and form between the above types and Jazz. Ragtime, the form most similar to Jazz, differs in several important respects:

1. Ragtime is predominantly a solo piano music, while New Orleans Jazz is predominantly ensemble music.

2. Ragtime has a syncopated homophonic structure while New Orleans Jazz retains the strong syncopation of the former, combined with a polyphonic texture.*

3. Ragtime, in terms of function, served as musical accompaniment in fixed locales, for example, social gatherings in the home, theaters and saloons.

4. Jazz, on the other hand, did not originally function in fixed locales, but was highly mobile, being used for balls, dances, parades, funerals, weddings, groundbreaking ceremonies, and riverboat entertainment. A music for all occasions, Jazz was utilized in situations calling for intimate social contact outside the nuclear family and on occasions and locales that precluded transport of the piano. This multifunctional role of Jazz is akin to that of African music. Equiano, a slave who managed to purchase his freedom, wrote in his autobiography:

> We are almost a nation of dancers, musicians, and poets. . . . Every great event . . . is celebrated in public dances which are accompanied with songs and music *suited to the occasion* (Author's emphasis). †

Why, however, did Jazz have its origins in New Orleans rather than in St. Louis, Chicago, or other cities? And why did Jazz originate and develop between 1890 and 1910 and not during another historical period? These and related questions cannot be answered without first looking

---

* References are to early New Orleans Jazz.

† Gustavus Vassa, *The Interesting Narrative of the Life of Olaudah Equiano* (London: T. Wilkins, 1789; New York: Frederick A. Praeger, 1966).

into the context of the social structure of New Orleans. In addition to being the birthplace of Jazz, New Orleans is also one of the oldest cities in the United States. Originally settled by Indians, New Orleans became thereafter the territory of Spain, France and, with the Louisiana Purchase in 1803, America. Even though territorial withdrawal was formalized by treaty, each national group left its distinctive cultural traits to the succeeding group vis-à-vis intermarriage or intermingling resulting in the polyglot ethnic-cultural mixtures that characterize the city. Before the Louisiana Purchase, the ethnic-cultural mixture of Spanish and French gave rise to a group termed *Creoles*. Very few if any Creole families were not also the product of African and/or Indian ancestry. Interbreeding was increased by *placage*, whereby the white male possessed a *concubinage* of two or more families mothered by both white and black females. The children fathered by such unions were half-brothers and half-sisters in effect, with many bearing a close physical and racial resemblance. Racial identification changed from being a matter of simple observation to one often requiring genealogical evidence. My thesis is that this biological integration, coupled with massive foreign immigration, led to intense competition and group identity crises. Jazz helped to create a sense of common cultural identity and uplift of morale in Afro-American communities where conditions had been made ripe for intra-group conflict.*

De Tocqueville is the first and, throughout the nineteenth century, the major exponent of the view that the modern regime is characterized by the *fragmentation of social class*, with the key elements dispersed in this fashion: power to the masses and to centralized bureaucracy, wealth to an ever-enlarging middle class, and status to the varied and shifting sectors of society which, in the absence of true class, become the theaters of the unending

---

* It is noteworthy that massive European immigration was encouraged shortly after the abolition of slavery, a period during which black labor was abundant and needful of employment.

and agonizing competition among individuals for the attainment of the marks of status.*

De Tocqueville's description fits well with social class-status shifts in New Orleans except for the concept of fragmentation. The latter term implies a breaking-off, or splintering, process; however, throughout the nineteenth century, the beginning of Americanization of New Orleans and (during the last quarter of the century) the gestation years of Jazz, a process corresponding more to a contraction of class categories (a decrease in categories) occurred, with increasingly disparate ethnic groups and greater numbers of people being fitted into fewer and fewer social groupings (horizontal expansion of categories). Rohrer and Edmonson state:

> From the very beginning of the Americanization of New Orleans a shift in the caste-class structure began to appear. . . . Up to the time of the Civil War, the direction . . . of the old south was towards the creation of two color (or racial) castes, with gradual depreciation of the distinction between slave and free Negroes together with augmentation of the social distance between Negroes and white. . . . In the generation and a half of Reconstruction, the social structure of New Orleans became a system of two racial castes of three classes each, and bitterness generated by the war and the carpetbag reconstruction led to more conflict, hostility and fear between the two racial castes, and to more repressive measures on the part of the white caste towards the Negro. . . . The tendency was toward a society in which every Negro would be politically and economically subordinate to every white. †

By 1850, northern European immigrations began to swell the ranks of the white lower and middle classes. Where in 1800 there had been two ethnic groups com-

---

* Alexis De Tocqueville, *Democracy in America* (New York: Alfred Knopf, 1945).

† Rohrer and Edmonson, *The Eighth Generation Grows Up* (New York: Harper & Row, 1960), pp. 19 ff.

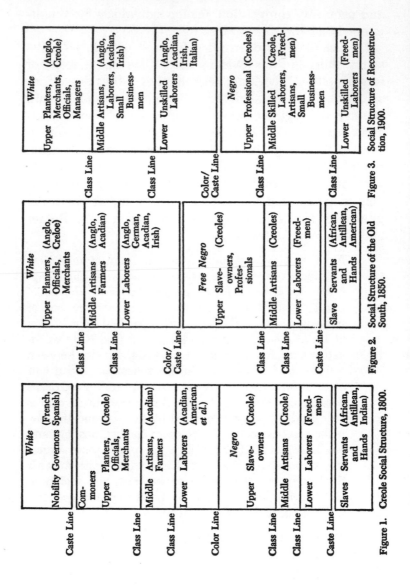

Figure 1. Creole Social Structure, 1800.

White		(French, Spanish)
	Nobility Governors	
Caste Line		
Com-moners		
Upper	Planters, Officials, Merchants	(Creole)
Class Line		
Middle	Artisans, Farmers	(Acadian)
Class Line		
Lower	Laborers	(Acadian, American et al.)
Color Line		
Negro		
Upper	Slave-owners	(Creole)
Class Line		
Middle	Artisans	(Creole)
Class Line		
Lower	Laborers	(Freed-men)
Caste Line		
Slaves	Servants and Hands	(African, Antillean, Indian)

Figure 2. Social Structure of the Old South, 1850.

White		(Anglo, Creole)
Upper	Planters, Officials, Merchants	(Anglo, Creole)
Class Line		
Middle	Artisans Farmers	(Anglo, Acadian)
Class Line		
Lower	Laborers	(Anglo, German, Acadian, Irish)
Color/ Caste Line		
Free Negro		(Creoles)
Upper	Slave-owners, Professionals	
Class Line		
Middle	Artisans	(Creoles)
Class Line		
Lower	Laborers	(Freed-men)
Caste Line		
Slave	Servants and Hands	(African, Antillean, American)

Figure 3. Social Structure of Reconstruction, 1900.

White		(Anglo, Creole)
Upper	Planters, Merchants, Officials, Managers	(Anglo, Creole)
Class Line		
Middle	Artisans, Laborers, Small Businessmen	(Anglo, Acadian, Irish)
Class Line		
Lower	Unskilled Laborers	(Anglo, Acadian, Irish, Italian)
Color/ Caste Line		
Negro		
Upper	Professional	(Creoles)
Class Line		
Middle	Skilled Laborers, Artisans, Small Businessmen	(Creole, Freed-men)
Class Line		
Lower	Unskilled Laborers	(Freed-men)

prising the white lower class, and one in the middle, by
1850, four ethnic groups were compressed into the lower
class and two instead of one in the middle. It is difficult
to know by the Edmonson table where the slave-owners
fitted; one can only assume that *planter* was a category
which included both slave-owning and nonslave-owning
planters. Whatever the case may be, it is sufficient to
note that after 1865 a slave-owning group undoubtedly
belonging to the upper class had lost many of its prerogatives and privileges, adding to the contraction and
compression of class structure in New Orleans. This was
the case for both the Anglo-Creole white group as well
as the nonwhite Creole group, even though, to judge by
Figure 2, only Free Men of Color or Free Negro Creoles
owned slaves. The period between 1865 and 1900 was to
have even more disastrous effects on Negroes, both Creole
and non-Creole, than on the white groups. For the Creole
of African ancestry, it meant a conversion of the laissez-
faire racial policy, whereby both Negro and white Creoles enjoyed equally high economic advantages and were
both considered aristocracy, to an either/or dichotomy
of two separate mutually exclusive racial classifications.
The former structure was derived not so much from social
egalitarianism, but from an attempt to deny the pervasive
effects of *placage* that made it impossible to claim the
fiction of pure race, and to create an atmosphere of social
and psychological distance in order to prevent collabora-
tion between Creoles and slaves that might lead to in-
surrection.*

As slavery came to an end, the 1850 social structure,
with its middle class of Creole artisans, swelled to include
former slaves who had skilled trades. It should be noted
that unlike the plantation slavery of the rural south, the
New Orleans system could be termed urban slavery, in
which construction, carpentry, plastering or metal working

* Henry Kmen, *Music in New Orleans* (Baton Rouge: Louisiana State
University Press, 1966).

were substituted for field labor. In addition to the artisans, the middle class began to include skilled laborers formerly of the lower class, and small businessmen—three categories where before there had been one.

Had there been a social scene in which the dominant white majority was not itself preoccupied by status, mobility and *status anxiety*, the problem for Negroes would have been a simpler one. The consequence was that Negroes could only appear as a threat to a white status already made fragile and uncertain by currents of European history that had little to do with them. But in his analysis De Tocqueville neglects the entire slave system, in which the Negro was very much involved, and the concomitant Reconstruction period, which saw class contractions and compression *within* the Negro group. This leads to a unidimensionality of *interracial* conflict-status anxiety, and a failure to conceptualize the equally important role of carefully manipulated *intraracial* status anxiety and conflict over identity. Negroes appeared not only as a threat to white status but to each other as well, after the slave caste was abolished and its members began to assume positions and status formerly held exclusively by the Free Men of Color, another name for Creoles of known Negro extraction.

Before 1865, the Catholic Church in New Orleans had made few distinctions according to race; the Free Men of Color and white Creole Catholics lived in the same downtown area and attended the same churches. However, the church which had offered a sense of belongingness to colored Creoles, on a par with whites, gradually began to conform to segregationist mandates following the Civil War, with the net result that two separate churches were formed, one for white groups and one for colored.* This process was completed in 1896 with the separate-but-equal statutes of the *Plessy v. Ferguson*

---

* In an interview conducted in New Orleans in 1971, Mr. R., a seventy-eight-year-old musician, noted: "A hundred years ago the Catholics baptized both whites and free Negroes of color. They wrote the names in the church records and after the Negroes' names they initialed the letters

Act. Blacks who were formerly Protestants joined the Catholic Church in increasing numbers, thus negating the exclusive status privileges held by the colored Creoles. Oretha Castle, a member of the New Orleans branch of CORE, describes the intraracial complexity and diversity of the city's Afro-American population:

> We don't have just Negroes. We have our Protestant Negroes, our Catholic Negroes, our downtown Negroes and our uptown Negroes, our light Negroes and our dark Negroes. . . . †

Few things that he observed in America struck De Tocqueville more forcibly and favorably than the profusion of associations that, in innumerable spheres, discharged social functions which in Europe were vested either in an aristocracy or in a political bureaucracy. "All societies require some degree of freedom of association," De Tocqueville wrote, "but nowhere is the need for 'intermediate associations' so great as in a democracy. . . . Associations serve the twin purposes, of providing a *haven for the individual* [italics mine], thus freeing him of the desire to seek absorption in the mass . . ." ‡ De Tocqueville differentiated clearly between political associations and civil associations; the former are manifest largely in political parties, the latter in the great profusion of social, cultural and economic associations. From the point of view of the vitality of the social order and of protection of the individual, the latter are the more important. By their very existence they reflect a high degree of individual social action and membership. This analysis fails, however, to explicate the relation-

F.M.C. which stood for Free Men of Color. Later when segregation came in, the families of these Negroes who had married their children off to white families, erased the initials after the names. You can still see the erasures and the faint initials F.M.C. At least 50 percent of the white families had some Negro blood, and I've heard people say as high as 90 percent. Most of the Negroes who decided on *passé blanc* left New Orleans where the fear of detection was minimized."

† "The Zulus," *New Yorker* magazine, June 20, 1964, p. 66.
‡ De Tocqueville, *op. cit.*, p. 118.

ships between democracy, the need for social identity and the functions of associations. Do democracies tend, by their emphasis on equality and class mobility, to produce alienation and, conversely, do nondemocracies produce social integration? De Tocqueville's analysis is, by itself, insufficient to explain why a similar profusion of civil associations did not occur in Europe during the same period.

However, by locating status anxiety as an independent variable and profusion of associations as dependent, one may more clearly differentiate the European from the American case. The independent variable, class stratification, can be seen in the former as a relatively fixed phenomenon and in the latter as a highly variable one moving in the direction from greater to fewer class categories, accompanied by a greater ethnic-racial clustering within class categories.

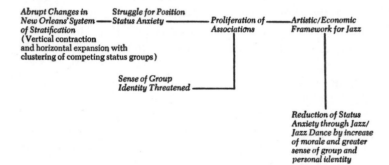

Associations then become the means by which status anxiety is reduced, which explains why New Orleans to a greater degree than other American cities saw the rise and organization of a multitude of social, cultural and economic associations. These associations were multifunctional, providing the community with sickness and accident insurance, death benefits—which included a funeral band—and, most important for our discussion, a means of intimate intra-ethnic social contact through numerous balls and dances, all of which rested on musical performances. Out of this social synthesis came a cumulative musical synthesis, which incorporated Spirituals, the syncopated elements of Ragtime, the brass and wind instrumentation of European band music, the voodoo aesthetic and many of the elements and formal arrangements of Blues.

Some of the group-supportive functions and aesthetic outgrowths of the New Orleans association are discussed by Alex Raphael, a member of the Zulu association. The Zulus, although founded as a carnival organization, have more in common with the traditional New Orleans burial society:

> The club is chiefly to be a help in the community. We have a room to meet in . . . and if a member is sick, we pay him so much a week. When he dies, he gets a band of music at his funeral. We have socials during the year. Carnival is just one project. . . . The white liberals love Zulu. The jazz buffs, and all, see it as part of a culture, something artistic.*

Until 1890 the music in New Orleans had primarily consisted of European-style band music with a syncopated beat, in addition to Ragtime piano, Spirituals, Blues and European dance music. None of the foregoing were adequate to meet the functional requirements of the new social gatherings. Marching bands were too unwieldy and their dependence on notated music did not lend itself to the need for hasty regroupings or the demands of alternating membership. The uptown non-Creole players, having been exponents of the nonnotated Blues, introduced improvisatory techniques, which on the one hand enabled the playing of extended compositions from "head" arrangements, and on the other hand facilitated ensemble playing by musicians with varying sight-reading abilities. † The polyphonic texture of New Orleans Jazz was, in turn,

---

* "The Zulus," *op. cit.*, p. 54.

† A "head" arrangement is one where thematic and harmonic materials are developed during rehearsal and memorized by the players for subsequent performances.

a resultant of an instrumentation whose functional requirements precluded the use of the piano.

Polyphony also provided a musical analogue to the new interdependence within the black community. All were now soloists, weaving their respective voices in a nonverbal form of social interaction and communication.

An examination of business cards of New Orleans Jazz musicians from 1890 to 1910 reveals a frequent use of the phrase, "Music for all occasions." The multifunctional character and services of New Orleans civic associations were thus transferred to a multifunctional music. The interchangeability of parts and instruments made possible by the art of improvisation and techniques of "head" arranging also go hand in hand with the aspect of multifunctionality.

Before 1890, European-derived dances such as the quadrille, polka, mazurka and waltz were performed at private balls. Mrs. Alice Zeno, the ninety-five-year-old mother of Creole clarinetist George Lewis, made the following statement during an interview with Marshall Stearns, Jazz critic and author:

> As a girl back around 1878, I danced the Mazurka, the polka, the Waltz, and of course, the Quadrille. I don't remember the Irish Reel and I certainly never danced the Slow Drag. . . . We had many lovely *Creole dances* and we danced in ballrooms by invitation only. Brass bands played for us—cornet, clarinet, and trombone— but no strings. My, but those *Creole dances* were elegant.

With the enactment of code No. 111 in 1894, forcing the Creoles into the uptown neigborhoods, and the 1896 separate-but-equal statutes, the subsequent amalgamation between Creole and non-Creole Negroes resulted in a stylistic synthesis called Jazz and a new set of dances— the slow drag, the buzzard lope and the eagle rock. Music and its corollary, the dance, became instrumental in reducing status anxiety by enhancing group identity through direct social participation that allowed for closer, less for-

malized contact between otherwise alienated
individuals. Whereas the European dances had
sized social distance disguised as elegance, the accent
now placed on close mutual contact. As Charles Love, born
in 1885, describes the slow drag: "Couples would hang
onto each other and just grind back and forth in one spot
all night."

"Raggy" strings, mainly the violin, were added to the
nuclear instrumentation of trumpet, trombone and clarinet, and with the "hot" fiddle, as it was called, the ensemble replaced the smooth, even, regular rhythms and
melodies with an uneven syncopated and more emotion-
ally intense music, which had appeal to all social strata.
Mr. G., age 70, a New Orleans Jazz bass player, made
the following comment to me in a taped interview (1971):

> When you listen to Jazz, you get a different type of beat;
> you have a chance to pat pat your hands, and it works
> your emotion a little bit, it gives you a warm feeling.
> When you listen to symphony, you listen to fine points,
> to the soloist. We used to think of the symphony boys
> as the long hairs. You have to have a taste for it to
> enjoy symphony, but you find that anybody on the
> street can enjoy Jazz, from the silk stocking boys on
> Charles Street to the ghetto boys.

Jazz, a musical synthesis, had its origins in the multifunctional requirements of associational gatherings. Closer
interpersonal contact and the beginning of intra-ethnic
cohesion resulted and reduced the level of status anxiety
brought on by change in social stratification after Reconstruction. The new and original music, Jazz, unlike its
musical predecessors, provided an oral and physical nexus
to the social participants of differential status, engaged
in the art of dance. Jazz, thus functioning as a social catalyst, had cross-status appeal to all sectors of black as well
as white society. Today, Jazz continues in New Orleans
and elsewhere to provide its audience with ties of shared
symbolic communication that transcend the hiatus of
color, race and status.

5

The Jazz Age:
Music of the Twenties and Thirties

Shake your brown feet, Liza
Shake 'em, Liza, chile,
Shake your brown feet, Liza
    (The music's soft and wil')
Shake your brown feet, Liza,
    (The banjo's sobbing low)
The sun's going down this very night—
Might never rise no mo'.
                    —Langston Hughes

During the Twenties, New Orleans was being phased out as a center of Jazz music. Many of its outstanding local players, including King Oliver, Louis Armstrong and Baby Dodds, were leaving for New York and Chicago, the new centers of the music industry. An inexorable process was gradually set into motion which steadily diminished the function and the importance of the locally based musician. His influence as musical model and social catalyst was to give way eventually to the monolithic dictates of a centralized industry. When a group of whites like the "*Original* Dixieland Jazz Band" succeeded in copying the external features of a particular black form or style, moves would be made by the industry to record, advertise and promote the "new" (and white) product. Others, including black musicians, would then be obliged to adopt the character of this white performance model in order to justify their professional competence.

> Chris Smith [Afro-American composer] had written [innovative] rags consisting of three sentimental ballads, a coon song and a waltz. The *New York Age* was more impressed with the imitators than it was with the creators. . . . Dozens of young white musicians with unabashed enthusiasm were trying to imitate the style of the Original Dixieland Dance Band. Not only was this group making a fortune through royalties on its records and tunes but they were getting as high as $1,000 a night for an engagement. . . . Of the Negro musicians trying to follow the new Jazz band craze, only Wilbur Sweetman, a clarinetist who had been touring vaudeville with his Ragtime Novelties, had much success.[*]

Following the vogues of the mechanical pianola, phonograph and radio, the generalized American audience, rather than the black community, the artistic spawning ground for black musicians, became the standard of audience acceptance. The phonograph especially was a boon to the mushrooming industry of prerecorded music, providing maximum profits with minimum costs. Now it was possible for one performance to be duplicated and reproduced almost endlessly by manufacturer and listener respectively. Only leaders and songwriters were in a legal position to realize payments or royalties from record sales. For the "sidemen" only one, the initial performance, was paid, although sales and therefore performances could run into the millions. "Hits" were the big payoff, since they allowed a company to conserve its financial resources by eliminating the need for continuous reinvestment in new talents and recordings. Soon what people wanted to hear became synonymous with what was selected or programmed for them to hear. The musical cartel stretched its boundaries to include music publishing, recording, distribution and

[*] Samuel B. Charters and Leonard Kunstadt, *Jazz: A History of the New York Scene* (New York: Doubleday, 1962), pp. 66, 68.

the radio media. Around the mid-Twenties, the gangster element made inroads into the industry, at first employing Jazz in "speakeasies" but also later venturing into the juke-box and distribution fields.

Babs Gonzales tells an interesting story of the Mafia takeover of the jukeboxes:

> I didn't see Mickey again for two years . . . when I returned to his town. The procedure was the same ex-cept he had now acquired three bars. One day I went by one of them and while I was there the complete front window was smashed. Everyone ducked for cover and when normality resumed, I asked him why all the violence. He told me that an Italian guy had sold him half interest in one hundred juke boxes and cigarette machines for thirty grand and the other mafia guys didn't want Negroes in that business.*

Jazz, unlike symphonic music, has never been gener-ously underwritten by private patrons of the arts, nor supported by public or quasi-public monies. From the New Orleans days on, the sale of liquor had helped to subsidize the sale of Afro-American music..

Like the present narcotics situation, prohibition meant extra-large profits for the underworld. The majority of night clubs and honky-tonks had to close down, but a series of clandestine operations called speakeasies quickly arose, which sold liquor illegally and often provided music. Since these were one of the few sources of steady employ-ment, musicians were hardly in a position to refuse the opportunity of working in them. Brothels run by Blacks, another source of employment for black musicians, were closed down in New Orleans and other cities during World War One. Houses like that of Marie Laveau, the New Orleans voodoo queen, catered to the wealthy, in-cluding many whites. The houses and honky-tonks were places where a relatively large amount of capital flowed

---

* Babs Gonzales, *I Paid My Dues* (New York: Lancer Books, 1967), pp. 83–84.

into the black community—that is, until official government decrees allowed takeover of these enterprises by immigrant ethnic gangster groups.

> On November 14, 1917, the mayor of New Orleans closed down Storyville on orders from the Secretary of the Navy, who apparently considered the tenderloin a sort of domestic torpedo aimed at the underbelly of the Armed Forces. While the madams removed their girls into better neighborhoods and quietly resumed trade, honky-tonk business slumped and the jazzmen were on the street. Many dropped out of the music business for good.*

From the Twenties to the present, the arm of the syndicate has remained around the neck and pocketbook of Jazz musicians and the black community's economic structure:

> Musicians in the middle 1920's frequently missed a beat when Al (Scarface) Capone or his brother Ralph or the handsome Dion O'Bannion and their henchmen paraded into a club and requested their favorite songs. The Capone headquarters was in nearby Cicero, in the suburbs, but the Capones as well as rival clans enjoyed night life and the excitement of loud, brilliant, slow and up-tempo jazz. Some of the speaks were owned outright by the hoods. Earl Hines said that his good friend Jimmie Noone as well as Lucky Millinder, Tiny Parham, and Boyd Atkins all were employed by the Capones at one time or another. †

Gone were the creative, affluent days of New Orleans, as many of its outstanding players left in search of work and the opportunity for a permanent career. The local scene was being usurped by an increasing tendency toward bureaucratic centralization of the music industry. The music, created and developed in New Orleans, was

---

* Alan Lomax, *Mister Jelly Roll* (New York: Grosset and Dunlap, 1950), pp. 179–180.

† Dave Dexter, Jr., *The Jazz Story* (Englewood Cliffs, N.J.: Prentice-Hall, 1964), p. 38.

now being sold back in the form of phonograph recordings and radio shows performed most often by white musicians.

Whites who were professional musicians now had a better opportunity to learn and imitate the external aspects of Afro-American musical models, given the large, ever-available supply of artificially produced "canned" music. As soon as the industry could come up with satisfactory imitations, new labels—such as "sweet" or "swing" —were born. Top radio and recording contracts went preferentially to white musicians, such as Goodman and Dorsey.

Radio broadcasting began in the early Twenties but it was not until 1928 that Jazz was to be performed on that medium, and then mostly by white bands such as those of Ben Pollack, Paul Whiteman and Rudy Vallee:

> Publishers of standard [European classical and semi-classical] music have adopted the recommendations of the Music Publishers Association of the U.S. and will allow "standard" music to be broadcast by radio without charge. This does not affect the stand taken by the American Society of Composers, Authors, and Publishers several weeks ago, forbidding radio stations to broadcast their music except upon payment of a license fee. Practically none of the jazz selections and popular songs will be radioed by the majority of the stations.*

There was no problem insofar as "standard" works were concerned, since standard meant, for the most part, pre-twentieth-century European compositions. The copyright laws pertaining to music did not come into being until 1909. They were not retroactive, being applied only to music composed after its passage. There was, before that, much litigation in the courts about song and performance rights in relation to radio. Out of the ferment came The American Society of Composers, Authors, and Publishers, or ASCAP, as it came to be known. This "non-profit" or-

---

* *The New York Times*, May 20, 1923, p. 12.

ganization acted as a clearing house, whereby licenses were granted to play songs under ASCAP rules for a "reasonable fee." By 1928 a settlement was worked out.

However, it mainly benefited those who had the greatest access to music-publishing firms and favorable contracts, and whose music was played most often on the radio. In both cases the musicians were white. ASCAP was open to any composer or author of a regularly published composition. The rub was in getting published, which has never been easy for whites and much less so for Blacks. The organization also protected the copyrights of publishing companies. In neither case were the interests of performer-composers protected. Unlike post-eighteenth-century European classical music, Afro-American music places a great emphasis on composition simultaneous with performance. The two are inseparable, due to the element of spontaneous improvisation. This holds true also for the performance of published material, since what may be termed recomposition occurs, wherein during each performance infinite variations in content may occur. This process was carried to its logical conclusion during the so-called bebop era, when harmonic structures from published songs were combined with new melodies (heads) followed by solo and ensemble improvisation. To this extent a Jazz player is also a composer, which also holds true for the instrumental aspects of Blues. To this day, "sidemen," the majority of performer-composers of Afro-American music, receive no royalties from any sector of the music industry. If the musician is a union member, which is usually the case for musicians who record, a single outright payment is made. The union's Music Performance Trust Fund, established in 1948 from contributions paid by record manufacturers based on volume of sales, is supposed to provide a substitute for royalties:

> They may be expended only to pay instrumental musicians for services, at local union scales, in performances open free to the public without charge, on occasions which, in the judgment of the Trustee based solely upon

the public interest, will contribute to the public knowledge and appreciation of music.*

These types of royalties usually depended more on political connections within the union than on either number of recordings made or musical ability. For the rank-and-file such engagements have always been rare. Since formerly separate black and white locals have "amalgamated," the situation has worsened in this and other respects for the Afro-American musicians, most Trust Fund jobs going to whites.

The growth of the music-recording industry is historically and parasitically connected with the growth of Jazz. The industry's growth was, and still remains, dependent on the grooming and packaging of white "popular" music models derived from imitations of definitive Afro-American models. It was not until the early Twenties, after the succession of music reproduction inventions and the advent of radio, that the music industry was fully able to capitalize on the use of white imitators!

> In 1921, United States production of records had exceeded 100,000,000 (a fourfold increase over 1911), and though the figure had dropped to 92,000,000 in 1923, there was still no cause for alarm. This prosperity was largely attributable to jazz, a form of music by then in full flower, though the original improvisatory jazz played by small ensembles had been submerged by a more commercial variety to which the whole country was dancing in new, gaudy ballrooms. †

Once the definitive Afro-American musical models have been studied and copied, with novelty effects added, the best imitators become white models and are then promoted nationally and internationally. The antecedents of cultural parasitism occurred well before the formal estab-

* Recording Industries Music Performance Trust Funds. Twenty-fifth Combined Reports and Statements of Trustees, Period 1 January 1961– 30 June 1961, p. 3.

† Roland Gelatt, *The Fabulous Phonograph* (Philadelphia: J. B. Lippincott, 1955), pp. 212–213.

lishment of "Tin Pan Alley." Eileen Southern notes that "Blackface minstrelsy was a form of theatrical performance that emerged during the 1820's and reached its zenith during the years 1850–70. Essentially it consisted of an exploitation of the slave's style of music and dancing by white men, who blackened their faces with burnt cork and went on the stage to sing Negro songs (also called Ethiopian songs), to perform dances derived from those of the slaves, and to tell jokes based on slave life." * John Tastes Howard reveals a similar process in the work of Stephen Foster: "It is interesting to compare the refrain of Stephen Foster's 'Camptown Races' with several other songs of the period. It is almost identical melodically with the Negro Spiritual 'Roll Jordan, Roll' and has its counterpart in music and text with the chantey, 'Doo-Dah-Day.'" † The white Jazz band which had most carefully observed the black New Orleans style was billed as the Original Dixieland Jazz Band, the creators of Jazz, and sent quickly off to Europe:

> They had learned the music of the Negroes in New Orleans, and they brought their "jazz" to Chicago, New York, London, and the world at large. Thus to a vast number of people, for quite a long time, the kind of music the Original Dixieland Jazz Band played represented all of jazz. Actually, the impression that this particular band was, in itself, a starting point is somewhat of an exaggeration. They were far from being the first jazz band, of course; were not even among the very first white bands, not the first to bring the music out of New Orleans and up North. But . . . they made the initial jazz recordings, in 1917. And . . . like many another group of their time, they went in for cowbells and other dubious "novelty" effects. ‡

* Eileen Southern, *The Music of Black Americans: A History* (New York: W. W. Norton, 1971), p. 100.
† John Tastes Howard, *The New York Times*, May 30, 1971.
‡ Orrin Keepnews and Bill Grauer, Jr., *A Pictorial History of Jazz* (New York: Crown, 1955), p. 19.

By the mid-Twenties sheer size itself was one of the novelties employed to establish the so-called big-band era. New Orleans Jazz ensembles were rarely larger than sextets or septets. They usually involved melodic instruments such as trumpet, clarinet, trombone and a rhythm section of bass, drums and guitar. Occasionally saxophones and violins were used. In many instances, when a greater variety of sound was desired the men would double or triple on other instruments, which was indicative of their skill and versatility. What Paul Whiteman, called by whites the "King of Jazz," did was to create visual novelty by forming sections of these basic instruments. Instead of one trumpet, there were now four; instead of one trombone there were now four, etc. New Orleans musical figures and nuances were imitated through written, arranged sectional riffs, often written by black arrangers. In other words there was little basic change in content from New Orleans Jazz, to sweet, to swing, only superficial changes in terms of novelty effects and identification labels:

> Prominent white orchestra leaders, concert singers and others were and still are making commercial use of Negro music in its various phases. That's why they introduced "swing" which is not a musical form.*

It appears that for very good reason many New Orleans Jazzmen, including Freddy Keppard and Tony Jackson, distrusted identification through written music arrangements and recordings; in short, anything that might undermine their products of originality and self-expression. Rumor has it that Victory Records offered Keppard a record date but he refused it. He didn't want his music copied. This sentiment among earlier artists was not uncommon. The master violin makers of Cremona took their secrets with them to their deaths.

In the Forties and Fifties white bands such as those of Stan Kenton, Woody Herman and Les Brown attempted

---

* W. C. Handy, *Father of the Blues* (New York: Macmillan, 1941), p. 304.

unsuccessfully to graft on visual and instrumental novelties from the Twenties and Thirties to the bebop content. The Kenton band in particular specialized in novelty effects such as extra-high trumpet playing and heavy-handed dissonance. In the contemporary era, the novelty effects are produced by electronic devices along with the rock identification label, although the basic content remains that of Afro-American Blues.

The relationship between promotion, advertising and the creation of white models in the Twenties and Thirties is not altogether different from that of today.

One of the few Afro-American models who managed to survive such an environment was Louis Armstrong. It can nevertheless be argued that he did so at considerable sacrifice to the New Orleans content and style that had exemplified his earlier playing. Armstrong recounted on "The David Frost Show" a revealing bit of advice given him by a white New Orleans businessman at a point when his career was just beginning to take shape: "Behind every successful Negro there is a white man." How could Armstrong not agree with him when so few black businessmen could invest in the music industry or pursue managerial or promotional careers?

Over the years Armstrong maintained his earlier technical standards of excellence, but his appeal to the mass audience no longer permitted the creative vigor that had hitherto characterized his work. White audiences (and most promotional work is aimed at white audiences) appreciated the image of the entertainer as much as, if not more than, his artistry. Artistic prowess becomes obscured and confounded with the notion of showmanship in such a setting. Lacking institutional supports and subsequent legitimation as high art, Jazz musicians past and present have had to adopt some form of entertainment posture. The following anecdote is revealing in this respect. A university administrator, referring to a Bay Area musician he was having difficulty remembering, said, "Now I know who you mean. Isn't he the one who wears the Russian hat? I just love those weird hats he always wears." *

Armstrong was known the world over for his warmth of personality, both on and off stage. The question is, had he not been so warm, might his career have been less illustrious, given the same degree of artistry? There has been a constant tension between the definitions of Jazz performer as artist, versus entertainer, and criteria of evaluation based upon artistic merit versus personality traits. The issue came to the surface during the Forties when Jazz musicians began to define themselves in terms of legitimacy and artistic value. Implicit was a recognition of the inherent social value of Jazz as a vehicle for the formation of group and personal identity. These functions are well expressed in the following excerpts from *Snakes:*

> Champ turned both me and Shakes on to some of the beautiful sounds that were floating around that we had never truly gotten into.
>
> Some of that music, Jazz mostly, really turned me around the first time I stopped and started listening to it. There are tunes that still conjure up the way I was feeling, the change that was coming over me in those lonely silly days. . . . This is some of what comes to mind when I think of those wild, impressive, heartbreaking days when I first began to thrive on sounds. Ideas, feelings, everything was connected to sounds, to song, a chord cluster, rapid-fire solo breaks, slow sneaky melody lines, counterpoint (which I read all about in the library listening to so called serious music). †

The issue of Jazz as art versus entertainment came to the fore in a recent and historically significant confronta-

---

* From an interview conducted in 1970 in Berkeley, California. With respect to the artist such behavior may be an expression of individuality. From the standpoint of audience, it may carry the meaning of social deviance which may be tolerated for its entertainment value beyond the value of the performance itself. Unfavorable career outcomes may result from the talented Jazz performer who chooses to forego such devices.

† Al Young, *Snakes* (New York: Dell, 1970), p. 36.

tion between Dick Cavett and the Jazz Pooples Movement:

> Cavett: What's causing this [lack of recognition of Jazz artists]? I have friends who are great Jazz buffs and some of them have stopped going to some of the Jazz places because they say the musicians are very hostile to the audiences and play with their back to them and a couple of other things and are really rough.
>
> Cecil Taylor: I thought we were talking about art. . . . There are those great artists, for instance, classical white artists who have their eccentricities and no one speaks about those eccentricities. They are immediately assimilated into the traditional attitude which has been propagandized by many great philosophers who have written about white artists—so everyone accepts that— why now, when a few, perhaps, black musicians turn their backs on the audience—why do people react to that? I think you go there to listen to the music.*

Managerial middlemen from cultures and ethnicities other than Afro-American were quick to seize upon the new opportunities afforded by the rise of the music industry:

> Joe Glazer was the Sunset's [a Chicago cabaret] aggressive, persuasive, baseball-crazy proprietor. He loved the games at nearby Comiskey Park, home of the White Sox, but he loved the trumpet style and income possibilities of Armstrong even more. He became his manager. . . . †

Non-Blacks like Glazer began controlling not only the reproduction of black music but also the black musicians. The biggest payoff, after the industry's portion, was to white musicians. Things have not changed very much over the past fifty years, for this is still the final result of technological combined with imitative process. For the most part, only the smaller companies would record Afro-

---

* From "The Dick Cavett Show," October 23, 1970.
† Samuel B. Charters and Leonard Kunstadt, *op. cit.*, p. 238.

American artists, while the large ones sought out the white bands.

Armstrong became successful, but the Twenties and Thirties were lean years for most other New Orleans Jazz pioneers, who refused to do the show biz antics that were required along with their skill in order to gain "success."

> Finally in the early thirties, [Jelly Roll] Morton and King Oliver realized that New York had beaten them. They each tried to find their way back to the life they had known before they came to the city, Jelly with his shabby night club in Washington and Oliver with a tragic series of one-night stands in the South.*

Despite formal regulations by amalgamated unions, the average Afro-American Jazz musician makes no more on a four- or five-hour job than in the Thirties. Five to ten dollars nightly is not unusual, nor is playing without any pay, for "exposure." In a recent interview conducted by the author, a formerly prominent New York City musician who is in the process of leaving the field stated: "I am happy that I am not in music because you have the same conditions and worse than ten, fifteen years ago." Many older black musicians (who pursued careers in the Twenties or Thirties and are still active professionally) would have probably added: You have the same conditions and worse as forty or fifty years ago! For, as the Jazz age drew to a close, many of the black musicians who, like Morton and Oliver, provided the stimulus, ethos and, above all, creative energy for this period (the longest period thus far in the twentieth century in which the United States has not been engaged in international warfare) were nonchalantly swept aside by the tides of technology, mechanical imitation, industrial monopoly, gangsterism, and the growing emphasis on showmanship and entertainment.

* *Ibid.*

6

Edward Kennedy Ellington: Contributions to Afro-American Culture

Boss, boss
tunes in
technicolor
  SOUL—
Black
Brown—
Beige—
Creole—
Black
  and
     Tan
is
the color
of my fantasy.
        —Sarah Webster Fabio,
        "Tribute to Duke"

For over fifty years, Edward Kennedy (Duke) Ellington and his orchestra have helped to keep alive the traditions of Afro-American culture. It would not be amiss to add that at times Ellington and his orchestra have developed and maintained almost singlehandedly a black cultural tradition. The intent of this chapter is to go beyond the mere recording of events and to strive for a synthesis of Ellington's contributions, describing how they tie in with the larger stream of Afro-American culture. At the same time I hope to derive some general formulations of the cultural meaning of Jazz for all music, both nationally and internationally.

It is almost unbelievable that Ellington has survived and prospered in a nation where commerce is often considered more important than art. Not only has he survived and prospered, but he is ". . . the unacknowledged but undeniable master of all Western music." * This fact of five decades of undisputed leadership justifies the "Duke" being elevated to "King," for Ellington, rather than Benny Goodman or Paul Whiteman, is the true king of black music. My thesis is that without Ellington, not only would a Goodman or a Whiteman have succumbed to the anti-artistic forces of American commercialism, but a large number of musicians, including many from the avant-garde school, would lack a model to follow. Composers of the European classical school owe a similar debt to Ellington. Stravinsky, Milhaud and Bernstein, whether they admit it or not, cannot escape the cultural imprint that Ellington has made and continues to make. The relationship between Euro-American classical composers and Jazz composers has traditionally been seen as proceeding in only one direction: classical music influencing Jazz. Leopold Stokowski is a rare exception to that tradition, for he reversed the direction of the relationship, stating that big bands are "America's most vigorous and original expression of the arts."

Ellington organized his first group shortly after World War One. At this time he first came into contact with the peculiarly American style of cultural exploitation. In his book *The Crisis of the Negro Intellectual*, Harold Cruse comments:

> . . . the role of the Negro, as entertainer . . . is still being used, manipulated, and exploited by whites (predominantly Jewish whites). Negro entertainment talent is more original than that of any other ethnic group, more creative ("soulful" as they say), spontaneous, color-

* Whitney Balliett, *The New Yorker* magazine, June 15, 1969.

ful, and also more plentiful. It is so plentiful, that in the marketplace of popular culture, white brokers and controllers buy Negro entertainment cheaply (sometimes for nothing) and sell it high—as in the case of Sammy Davis. But there is only *one* Sammy Davis. In the shadows, a multitude of lesser colored lights are plugging away, hoping against hope to make the Big Time, for the white culture brokers only permit a few to break through—thus creating an artificial scarcity of a cultural product. This system was established by the wily Broadway entrepreneurs in the 1920's. Negro entertainment posed such an ominous threat to the white cultural ego, the staid Western standards of art, cultural values and aesthetic integrity, that the entire source had to be stringently controlled.*

Despite the harsh realities of American commercialism, Ellington's orchestra is the only one, black or white, to survive without interruption for fifty years.

Let us look into some specific socio-economic aspects of this control as it affected Ellington. In the Twenties, when the new Ellington orchestra was struggling to remain intact, Irving Mills became Ellington's manager and good financial things began to happen. This fact alone presents a sad commentary on American society and its commercialism, for the implication is that without a white financial wizard the orchestra might have folded.

Ellington's first big job under his new manager was at the Cotton Club in New York. This was a white-owned club which was formerly called the Holiday Cafe. Like other white-owned clubs—for example, the Club Alabam in New York and the Plantation Club in Chicago—the Cotton Club promoted with all its force and ingenuity the image of the perpetually happy Negro. Ironically, the Cotton Club, although located in Harlem, was closed to Blacks except for a few celebrities, who were seated in the rear.

The motif of the club was a jungle and Ellington was

* *The Crisis of the Negro Intellectual* (New York: Morrow Paperback Editions, 1971), p. 109.

hired to play "jungle music." Marshall Stearns, a music
critic, wrote:

> I recall one [show] where a light-skinned and magnifi-
> cently muscled Negro clad in an aviator's helmet,
> goggles, and shorts burst through a papier-mâché jungle
> onto the dance floor. He had obviously been forced
> down in darkest Africa, and in the center of the floor he
> came upon a white goddess clad in long tresses and be-
> ing worshipped by a circle of cringing "blacks." Produc-
> ing a bull whip from heaven knows where, the aviator
> rescued the blonde and they did an erotic dance. In the
> background, Bubber Miley, Tricky Sam Nanton, and
> other members of the Duke Ellington band growled,
> wheezed and snorted obscenely.*

Stearns's description suggests the racist caricatures that
return to open prominence in the country (probably) as
a reaction to the level of equality Blacks had attained
during the war both at home and at the front; it was necessary to put "the negro" back into his proper place.

The black music that later became known as Jazz came
into being after Reconstruction governments were destroyed and represented to some degree a protest against
the systems of racial oppression and the lack of democracy
in America. By the early nineteen-hundreds Jazz had developed into definite forms and instrumental techniques.
In the period after World War One white business interests
began to take control of the artistic product. The names of
the bands of this period reveal their derogatory character
and suggest the racial exploitation that was introduced.
Such names as "McKinney's Cotton Pickers," "Sidney
Bechet's New Orleans Feet Warmers" and "The Lazy
Levy Loungers" diverted attention from the character
that Jazz music had originally reflected. "McKinney's Cotton Pickers" had formerly been known as "The Synco Jazz
Band." According to one member, the booking agent introduced the new name while suggesting that the former

* Marshall Stearns, *The Story of Jazz* (New York: New American Library, 1958), p. 133.

name lacked "originality." At the time of his Cotton Club engagement, when Ellington referred to his group as "The Famous Duke Ellington Orchestra," he registered a protest against the prevailing attempts at racial exploitation. Playing a typically dissonant chord at the piano, the Duke once pointed out, "That's the Negro's life, hear that chord. That's us. Dissonance is our way of life in America. We are something apart, yet an integral part." *

Nevertheless, Ellington's characteristic ability to turn every situation to his and the orchestra's advantage enabled him to profit artistically from the Cotton Club experience. He was one of the first composers to effectively orchestrate beyond the thirty-two-bar, ensemble-solo-ensemble pattern (i.e. the group plays the theme, a member or members solo, then the group comes in playing the theme again). He experimented with new orchestral colors and techniques while developing a broader conception of Jazz as a medium of artistic expression. His audience was greatly enlarged through the nationwide radio hookup with the Cotton Club.

During the Cotton Club engagement Ellington first conceived the idea of a Jazz opera. This conception crystallized many years later in his "Black, Brown and Beige" suite, first performed in 1943, and also in "My People," performed in 1963 in Chicago for the Century of Negro Progress Exposition.

Paradoxically, the Cotton Club experience helped Ellington break out of the racist network imposed by white business. While it attempted to restrict black music to the entertainment sphere, Ellington demonstrated on a national scale that Jazz, in addition to being "hot," could be lyrical, complex, plush and socially meaningful. Ellington proved that Jazz did not need to be restricted to night clubs or dance halls but could rightfully occupy its place as America's indigenous art form. No other artist, white or black, did as much as Ellington to demonstrate this.

* Barry Ulanov, *Duke Ellington* (New York: Creative Press, Inc., 1946), p. 276.

The period when Ellington was based in Harlem coincided with massive migrations from the South to the North. The graphs below illustrate this population movement. The center of black music shifted from New Orleans to New York. Subsequent to this population movement there was a flowering of black culture which became known as the "Harlem Renaissance."

Black Population

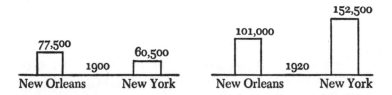

Unfulfilled promises of equal opportunity had created a deep pessimism among black people after the Reconstruction period. Black leaders struggled to overcome the repressive effects of the post-Reconstruction period with a variety of action programs. Booker T. Washington in the South began stressing the need for acquisition of basic skills and economic self-development, while W. E. B. Du Bois, a Northerner, wrote of the "talented tenth," an intellectual movement aimed at providing leadership for Blacks. Marcus Garvey took some of Washington's basic ideas and built a mass political movement based on separation of the races and a return by black people to Africa. Yet another idea was introduced: If both whites and Blacks could be educated to the black man's worth, discrimination could be ended once and for all. It was this idea that gave the Harlem Renaissance its motive force.

In the Twenties and Thirties, Harlem was a mecca for black music, poetry, history and education. Poets Langston Hughes and Claude McKay, poet and historian James Weldon Johnson and educator Alain Locke were some of the men who quested after a sense of black identity. They realized that without a sense of distinct black culture there could be neither economic nor political growth for Blacks.

During the Harlem Renaissance, Ellington wrote works dedicated to black cultural heroes:

"Black Beauty" (Florence Mills)—1928
"Portrait of the Lion" (Willie "The Lion" Smith)—1939
"Bojangles" (Bill Robinson)—1940
"A Portrait of Bert Williams"—1940

Bill "Bojangles" Robinson was a famous black tap dancer whose career spanned the generation from the early Twenties to the early Forties. Bert Williams was a well-known black comedian and actor, and Willie "The Lion" Smith was a famous black pianist. Ellington dedicated "Black Beauty" to Florence Mills, a singer and actress whose talents were much appreciated in the Broadway musical comedy field. By calling her black, even though she was of light complexion, Ellington anticipated by over thirty years the present-day, proud use of that term.

"My men and my race are the inspiration of my work," he has written. "I try to catch the character and mood and feeling of my people. The music of my race is something more than the American idiom. It is the result of our transplantation to American soil and it was our reaction in plantation days, to the life we lived. What we could not say openly we expressed in music. The charactertistic, melancholic music of my race has been forged from the very white heat of our sorrow and from our gropings." *

Without a doubt, Ellington was as much influenced by the Harlem Renaissance as he was a power in exerting influence upon it. He composed numerous works using Harlem as a motif. (See Discography, page 90.) He owned one of the largest collections of books dealing with Afro-America, and inculcated into his works themes on Blacks. He attempted to change the word *Jazz* to *Negro music* because the former word had become derogatory by implication—originally spelled *jass*, it suggested New Orleans bordello activity. Although Ellington was unable to

* G. E. Lambert, *Duke Ellington* (New York: A. S. Barnes and Company, 1959), p. 22.

bring about this change, some writers nowadays employ the term *Black music,* or *Afro-American music,* representing a partial and long overdue success for Ellington's efforts.*

By 1932 Ellington, reacting to his mother's death and the intense forces of white commercialism, entered a period of deep personal depression. When he took his compositions to publishers he often received a negative response:

> When I'd bring something I thought was good to the music publishers, they would ask, "Can an eight-year-old child sing it?" or "This ain't what we're looking for, we want something good." I thought I'd stop writing. Music publishers would come around with little tunes and say, "If you'll put your name on it, we'll make it our number one plug"! If something bad was plugged, it would go over better than something good that wasn't. I felt it was all a racket. I was on the point of giving up. †

Some periodicals of the period even stated that Ellington was not a good pianist, which, to them, explained why he divided his time between conducting and playing. These critics missed the point, since Ellington's compositions were evolving, becoming more complex; hence, more conducting was required to achieve balance and the varied tonal colorations he envisioned. The critics also focused careful attention on a mistaken dichotomy between Jazz and "longhair," or "serious," music. The assumptions underlying their statements were that Jazz, even Duke's, could never approach the artistic distinction that symphonic works had, and that Jazz was not intended for, nor, by implication, was it capable of, any serious purpose.

---

* Various terms used to describe Afro-American classical music have either been invented or given wide circulation by white critic-musicologists. Although the term *Jazz* continues to be associated with aspects of deviance, it has also found its way into the American vernacular (e.g., *Jazzy*) as an expression denoting spirit, imagination and excitement. It would seem, however, that by common assent of the musicians the term *Jazz* could be changed.

† *The New Yorker* magazine, July 8, 1944.

The period of Duke's depression coincided with the origins of so-called swing music and the ascendancy of the bands of Benny Goodman and Paul Whiteman. Ellington's orchestra had been tagged a "sweet" band, and even though Whiteman and Goodman had borrowed liberally from the Ellington tradition, the new term "swing" was like a new brand name—you must dig it in order to be "in." To counteract the danger of becoming outdated by a word, Duke's publicity staff had to convince the public that the Ellington orchestra *was* a "swing" band.

Like many other black artists of this and subsequent periods, Ellington was forced to go to Europe for recognition. In 1933 he took the band on a tour of England and the European continent. Wherever they went they were accorded a recognition hitherto unattained in the land of their birth.

As a result of Ellington's unprecedented and successful European tour, Jazz began to find its way into the symphonic idiom. Many European composers such as Milhaud, Honegger, Poulenc and others less well known began to incorporate Jazz into their compositions. In America composers such as Stravinsky began to use the melodic and rhythmic content of Jazz; the "Ebony Concerto" Stravinsky wrote for Benny Goodman is an example of this influence and owes a debt to Ellington for its inspiration.

Once recognized by European audiences and composers, Ellington found the way paved for broader acceptance at home, and he began to acquire more confidence in his compositional prowess. The exoticism of the Cotton Club period began to fade and he concentrated on a more supple, more sophisticated orchestral language. Ellington devoted himself to his music with tremendous energy and creativity.

It is almost axiomatic that any Jazz orchestra in America not financed by night clubs or private subsidies will likely fail financially. To keep his orchestra of top-quality musicians together, Ellington began to tour America extensively in a series of one-nighters. The high-spending days of the Twenties had passed and only white bands such as Whiteman's or Goodman's were given long-term contracts in night clubs or hotels. But there was another reason for the great amount of road travel and one-nighters which is best expressed in Ellington's own words:

> What I'm involved in is a continuous autobiography, a continuous record of the people I meet, the places I see change. Furthermore what is music if it isn't communication? I like to know firsthand what the response is to what I write. . . . By playing one-nighters I can hear reactions from all kinds of audiences. You get a real contact when you play a phrase and somebody sighs.*

Duke incorporated the images of his travels into his compositions. Billy Strayhorn, Ellington's arranger and confidant, once remarked that Ellington ". . . is continually renewing himself through his music. He's thoroughly attuned to what's going on now."

Everyday sounds, sounds that most of us take for granted, become the motifs and content of Ellington's music. This leads to the direct infusion of cultural and social-historical elements into his work. His own description of one of his many works on Harlem, "Harlem Air Shaft," indicates his sensitivity to his surroundings and suggests the influence this has upon his music. "So much goes on in a Harlem air shaft," he wrote. "You hear fights, smell dinner, hear people making love. You hear intimate gossip floating down. You hear the radio. An air shaft is one great big loudspeaker; you hear people praying, fighting and snoring." † Thus Ellington became a new type of Jazz composer, a composer who writes not merely for specific functions or a mass of people but for human beings with unique, distinctive characteristics. He composes with the individuality of each person of his audience in mind.

Ellington also composes for the individual artists in his orchestra, adapting his music to their unique personalities

---

* *The Reporter* magazine, May 7, 1964, p. 47.
† Duke Ellington, "Harlem Air Shaft," R.C.A. Victor record jacket notes.

and styles of performance. The individual personalities of his audience and the distinctive talents of the artists in his orchestra are the two major sources of Ellington's creative genius. Many other bands reflect only the leader's whims and personality, but the Ellington orchestra is not so singly motivated. This is why listening to the Ellington orchestra is a unique experience. His style of writing and performing gives the final composition a dynamic, improvised sound rather than the static sound that usually accompanies most symphonic works. He has insightfully remarked that so-called classical composers rarely hear their own works more than once or twice. Since symphony orchestras are not at their complete disposal, composers do not get a chance to try out different effects and techniques. Only when one of their works is being rehearsed or performed do they really know what they have written. Ellington gets continuous, immediate feedback on his works both from his audiences and from the members of his orchestra.

Though Ellington seldom leaves his music for other causes, he occasionally defends Jazz against its critics. In 1944, for example, *American Mercury* published an article, written by a Mr. Sargent, accusing Jazz of having no intellectual complexity, of lacking creative ingenuity and technique and of being restricted to four or five monotonous patterns. Sargent used the Blues to support his accusations. Duke responded in a letter to the editors: "Everyone knows that the Blues is built upon a set pattern, as is, for example the sonnet form in poetry. Yet this hasn't seemed to limit poetry to four or five monotonous patterns, nor do I think jazz is so limited." *

The critics have often been harsh despite the large following that Duke has built. "A Drum Is a Woman," written for a television special in 1957, was reviewed as flimsy and not up to Ellington's usual style. "Black, Brown and Beige" was described in a *Newsweek* magazine article in 1963 as brilliant, complex and highly original, but much

* *American Mercury* magazine, January, 1944.

too long. One cannot avoid the thought that these same critics would not oppose a Beethoven symphony or a Wagner opera because of length.

The most emphatic indictment of narrow-mindedness and racial bigotry in the arts was the refusal of the 1965 Pulitzer Prize Committee to grant Ellington the Pulitzer Prize. A partial list of American composers who had previously received this award is revealing: 1960, Elliot Carter; 1961, Walter Piston; 1962, Robert Words; 1963, Samuel Barber. They are without exception the heirs to European traditions and, as such, they copy another culture. In 1965 no prize was offered to a musician, a discreet but obvious way of avoiding public pressure against the racist policies of the Pulitzer Committee. In 1966 the prize went to Leslie Basett, in 1967 to Leon Kirchner, in 1968 to George Crumb. Not one of the composers honored by the Pulitzer Committee has been as prolific as Ellington, who has written over 2000 works, utilizing nearly every musical form. Nor have the Pulitzer-honored composers matched Ellington's contributions to American music in style and originality. When, in 1965, the Duke was informed of the Committee's decision not to award a prize in music, he remarked with characteristic aplomb, "Fate's being kind to me. Fate doesn't want me to be famous too young." He was then sixty-four years old.

Perhaps one of the reasons Ellington's remark was not more cutting is the fact that those who control the industry often boycott an artist who speaks out. Several musicians—for example Max Roach, Arthur Davis and Charles Mingus—have narrowly missed being thrown out of the performing role by record companies and club owners who resent a musician who thinks for himself and makes statements that go against the status quo.

The essence of Afro-America that Ellington captures in his music is suggested by the titles of his works incorporating black themes. Consider, for example, the following list, containing some of the best works he has ever written:

"Black and Tan Fantasy"—1927
"Creole Love Call"—1927
"Creole Rhapsody"—1931
"Ebony Rhapsody"—1934
"Black Butterfly"—1936
"Sepia Panorama"—1940
"Black, Brown and Beige"—1943
"Creamy Brown"—1943
"New World A-coming"—1943
"Liberian Suite"—1947
"Deep South Suite"—1947
"Harlem"—1951
"My People"—1963
"La Plus Belle Africaine"—1966

He has also composed works commemorating black freedom fighters:

Denmark Vesey—circa 1944
Nat Turner—circa 1944
Crispus Attucks—circa 1944
Harriet Tubman—circa 1944
Frederick Douglass—circa 1944

None of the latter group have been recorded, since the record industry is not concerned with portraying black history as much as with making a profit. Nevertheless, Ellington stands out as America's foremost composer.

His achievements, meriting his position as leader of American music, can best be measured by the statements of contemporary musicians. Miles Davis has said, "I think all musicians in jazz should get together on one certain day and get down on their knees to thank Duke." Cecil Taylor, an avant-garde pianist and composer, appreciates Ellington from two perspectives: "Whenever I get in the hole for ideas, one of the sources I go to is Ellington's conception of how to create colors. Also he showed me how it was possible to incorporate all kinds of musical and other influences as part of my life as an American

Negro. Everything Duke lived is in his music." Similar
statements by many contemporary Jazz artists could be
compiled.

The conclusion is inescapable. Ellington stands out not
only as America's foremost composer but as a great Afro-
American whose devotion to his people continues to give
us all great inspiration.

I Guess They'll Miss Me When I've Gone

Ellington's critics have sometimes been complimentary.
However, Paul Hertelendy revealed European chauvinism
and a raw disdain for that which is dissimilar in his review
of Ellington's performance with the San Francisco Symphony on August 10, 1968. The title of the review is revealing: "Jazz, Symphony in Shot Gun Wedding."

> Ellington is one of the grand old squares of jazz, a man
> who has repeatedly emerged at the top of the heap over
> some 40 years of music. Who else can lay that claim in
> these changing times? His program Saturday was a
> traditional Ellington with a lot of swing, symphonic tone
> poems in jazz idioms and old Ellington niceties like
> "Mood Indigo," "Sophisticated Lady," "Solitude." But
> jazz and symphony never consummated their union. . . .
>   The Duke brought along a threesome of his own men
> [Johnny Hodges, Jeff Castleman and Rufus Jones] that
> took a lot of pressure off the symphonists, who were
> having to masquerade as jazz men. . . . Some of the
> symphonists were uncomfortable in the Ellington mood,
> but not so, concertmaster and occasional conductor
> Joseph Krachmalnick, who obviously knew that it don't
> mean a thing if it ain't got that swing—and he swung
> from the heels . . .
>   The more symphonic the Duke's music became, the
> less successfully it projected.*

One could question why the entire Ellington orchestra
was not invited to perform.

* Paul Hertelendy, "Jazz, Symphony in Shot Gun Wedding," *Oakland
Tribune*, August 12, 1968.

The acceptance of Ellington among Blacks has at times been ambivalent. For example, when Dr. Marvin Chachere, a black director of the Letters and Science Extension, University of California at Berkeley, arranged a symposium and concert for Ellington entitled "The Great 'Duke' Ellington" (September 28–29, 1969), the attendance at the symposium did not include many Blacks. One of the symposium speakers who later reviewed the concert observed that it was difficult to speak of black pride in Ellington since he could "barely see a Black in the audience this morning."

Later in his review he remarked:

> There was not the number present there I would have liked to have seen. . . . But I rationalized that had this been someone of a more commercial nature, like James Brown or Aretha Franklin, or any number of present day favorites, the place would have been filled to capacity. . . . But I don't feel that the aforementioned have any more pride coming from the black community than Ellington. . . . On the contrary, they are just a bit more popular than Ellington: one of the reasons being the average listener today can understand the music emanating from the aforementioned, . . . it is music that is for the black man and woman. . . .
>
> Ellington's music, on the other hand, is for the white community. It always has been. . . . He has never had to say it, nor do I believe he intended to make it that much of a fact. Why should he? The mere fact that it was able to communicate black America; the rhythm, the mood, the anguish, the love, the indefatigable drive for equality was for white America to try and understand . . . and if it has seemed complex to most jazz, or soul enthusiasts, it has never been so to whites. . . .*

He quotes an eighteen-year-old black youth as having said the following about Ellington:

> I didn't find that I could dance to his music. And I couldn't listen to it; listen to it and understand it. I really

* "Jazz Scene," *Soul* magazine, December 1, 1969, p. 4.

> didn't think he was modern enough . . . but Duke is
> still a bad cat just the same. He's a black man that's
> done a lot. He has contributed greatly to Black culture
> and to the culture in America. For that I dig him.*

It is difficult to imagine that the youth would have made
the remarks about the lack of modern qualities of Ellington's music if the educational system had devoted the
same attention to the preservation and development of
appreciation of all eras of Afro-American classical music
as it devotes to appreciation of its masters of European
classical music.

Currently, the press appears to be even more unfavorable to this ever-prolific composer and musical genius.
Despite the fact that symphony orchestras usually have a
standard repertoire which they play year in and year out,
one reviewer expected more of Ellington:

> Duke Ellington's annual August visit to the Rainbow
> Grill, where he appears with a small group drawn from
> his full orchestra, can usually be counted on by Elling-
> ton followers as an opportunity to hear the Duke depart
> from the *set routine* he has been following in his con-
> cert appearances during the previous year.
>
> But apparently that is not to be the case this August.
> Mr. Ellington opened his four-week stand at the Rain-
> bow Grill on Monday evening with a condensed version
> of his *standard* concert program played by a smaller
> version (eight pieces) of his regular orchestra. . . .
>
> Half of the program was devoted to the singing of
> Miss Brookshire and Tony Watkins, a disappointing
> balance for anyone who had come to hear Mr. Ellington
> and his musicians. And it is even more disappointing
> to find Mr. Ellington doggedly ending even this pro-
> gram with his banal "one more time," the tawdry dis-
> play he insists on using to bring his regular concerts to
> a conclusion on a sour note (emphasis the author's). †

* *Ibid.*

† John S. Wilson, "Ellington Changes Format on Return to Rainbow
Grill," *The New York Times,* August 4, 1971.

Ellington's performance at the 1971 Newport Festival was criticized as follows:

> A lackluster set by Duke Ellington contributed to a mediocre evening of music for a Newport opener. The Duke, in a blue-striped suit, played more piano than usual in "Afro-Eurasian Eclipse," a segment of "New Orleans Suite" and Billy Strayhorn's "Take the A Train," full of brawn and barking brass.*

When will Edward Kennedy Ellington really be treated as a duke? Is he ever to receive the rewards of more comfortable performance conditions which befit his stature and contributions to America's oldest original art form— Jazz? This gifted individual deserves a concert hall where his orchestra can perform in residence. Since cities help underwrite the cost of civic symphonies to perform a European art form, Ellington's orchestra should be granted equal status. For example, funds from a city, from the National Endowment for the Arts and from several appropriate private foundations could be combined to provide the required financial support. New York City or Washington, D.C., his native city, are excellent possible locations. Lincoln Center or the new Kennedy Center for the Performing Arts (in Washington) are possible sites. Or a new center bearing Ellington's name could be erected just for Ellington's orchestra to perform there in residence.

Although Ellington has been given numerous honorary awards and citations, he has yet to receive support for the maintenance of his orchestra, and the permanent facilities to carry out his work with a minimum of frustration, as are European composers, conductors and musicians. He should be provided the special facilities which would subsequently allow him to work without the hindrances of tedious road traveling for "one-nighters" or weekly engagements in night clubs. Unfortunately, racist America

---

* Martha Sanders Gilmore, "Newport 1971 Festival Debacle," *International Musician*, August 1971, p. 8.

continues to seem unwilling to show genuine appreciation
for its black musicians until they have died.

Selective Ellington Discography

Compositions Using Black Cultural Motifs

"Black and Tan Fantasy"	Br 02306
"Creole Love Call"	HMV X 4957 and DLP 1094
"Black Beauty"	Br 02306
"Creole Rhapsody"	Br 01145
"Black, Brown and Beige Suite"	Worksong Vi 28-0400, Come Sunday Vi 28-0401-A, The Blues Vi 28-0401-B
"Ebony Rhapsody"	Vi 24622, 24674
"My People"	Contact CS1
"New World A-coming"	Vi disks issued during World War II
"Deep South Suite"	Not available
"Sepia Panorama"	Vi 26731

Compositions Dealing with Harlem as a Theme

"Echoes of Harlem"	Br 7650
"Blue Harlem"	Br 6374
"Drop Me Off at Harlem"	Co 35837, Br 6527
"Harlem Speaks"	Co 36195, Br 6646
"Harlem Air Shaft"	Vi 26731
"Harlem Mania"	Vi 38045, Bb 6306
"Jungle Night in Harlem"	Vi 23022, Bb 6335
"Harmony in Harlem"	Br 8044
"Harlem Flat Blues"	Br 02003
"Harlem Twist"	OK 8638
"Take the A Train"	Vi 27380

Compositions Dedicated to Famous Black Personalities

"Bojangles" (Bill Robinson)	Vi 26644
"A Portrait of Bert Williams"	Vi 26644

Selective Ellington Discography (continued)

"Portrait of the Lion"
  (Willie "The Lion"
  Smith)
"Black Beauty"
  (Florence Mills)

Abbreviations Used in Discography

Bb—Bluebird	OK—Okeh
Br—Brunswick	Vi—Victor
Co—Columbia	

7

"Bebop": The Music
That Was Forced Underground

I am the rhythm of my past, my present.
I sing a song of future. I shall sing my song.
— Eugene Redmond

When current values are challenged and assaulted by new
ones, a society is headed toward change. What was good
is no longer good; what was acceptable is no longer acceptable. Culture can be likened to a central set of values,
beliefs, customs and symbols from which radiate political
and economic institutions, as well as forms of social behavior. A change in the center effects change on the out-
lying perimeters. Values, the premises upon which culture
is formed, when redefined suggest and help activate al-
ternative customs and beliefs in addition to new sets of
behavioral norms. Art, the symbolic integration of custom,
belief and value, can be an aid in their maintenance, or it
can precipitate their change. In other words, the artist is
capable not only of creating works of art, but also new
social and artistic values embodied in his art.

Such a situation may often be viewed as a threat to
society, since the artistic expression of fundamental value
change is by definition a highly individualized action. By
acting on new value premises the artist is by implication
opposed to those values which find common acceptance:
forcing change, as it were. Established authority, which
institutionalizes and legitimizes those values deemed es-

sential to its goals, will react when it becomes clear that individual actions are having a collective impact. The artist is then viewed somewhat as an anarchist, as one who spreads terror and subversion rather than "art," and is treated accordingly.

From its inception bop was a challenge (and thus a threat) to the established order. To the uninitiated, not only was the music weird, but also the makers of the music. They "talked funny," and to the horror of agents, shunted aside popularity, conventional etiquette and monetary rewards in favor of a religious devotion to creative endeavors.

Bop came about during the deterioration of the intimate connection between Jazz and dance. From early slave days, dance had been an important part of Afro-American culture, and from the beginning these dances were received in ambivalent terms by whites. An editorial from the *Musical Courier* of 1899 suggests the nature of anti-dance sentiment that continues to pervade some circles:

> Society has decreed that ragtime and cake-walking are the thing, and one reads with amazement and disgust of historical and aristocratic names joining in this sex dance, for the cake is nothing but an African *danse du ventre*, a milder edition of African orgies.*

There are accounts of voodoo dances being banned in Congo Place, New Orleans. In these dances, unlike European dance, emphasis is most often placed on pelvic movements which are symbolic of the acts of fertility. A double threat was posed by such a dance. It was on the one hand a threat to the Protestant ethic of puritanism, hard work and devotion to material acquisition, and on the other hand threatened a social fabric based on racial exclusiveness. Black dances that turned into crazes, particularly during the Twenties and Thirties (as was the case in the sixties), often involved, as did their earlier voodoo predecessors, whites as participants.

* Marshall Stearns, *Jazz Dance* (New York: Macmillan, 1968), p. 123.

The Afro-American dance had grown from an intra-ethic cultural expression, as in New Orleans voodoo and Jazz secular dance, to a national craze with interethnic and interracial implications.

> In the early Thirties people had very little to celebrate; they felt vulnerable and as much as anything, wanted to be soothed. One could take a date to the movies, or just stay home for an evening and dance to radio music, but there came a time when you wanted to get out and be with others. The big social events were apt to be the dances, especially if you were of high-school age. Until the jukebox took over later in the decade, a few live musicians were necessary to provide the music. All over the country, in the small towns, you might hear "Are you going to the dance?" and "Who are you taking?" in anticipation of the coming weekends and holidays. Later in the decade (around the beginning of World War II) we were beginning to believe the Depression was on its way out; we felt a sense of release, and welcomed the big bands and the new dances with an excitement and exuberance unmatched in the Twenties and the later decades. . . . If you were lucky enough to be in New York City, you visited the temple of swing, the Savoy, up in Harlem.*

Dance bands became the rage. Ellington put it graphically and succinctly when he said, "It don't mean a thing if it ain't got that swing." Although there were many white bands, few really swung. Swing simply could not be located along the dimensions of European notational devices. Writing two or four quarter notes per measure, the closest that Western notation came to approximating the swing beat, was far removed and no substitute for it.

> The big dance bands (white) had carried off the healthiest child of Negro music and starved it of its spirit until its parents no longer recognized it. In defiant self defense, Negro players were developing something

* Don Congdon, *The Thirties, A Time to Remember* (New York: Simon & Schuster, 1970), pp. 356–357.

new—"Something they can't play," [Thelonius] Monk
once called it.*

What Monk failed to mention, however, was the concomitant need by the industry for "new" models to copy
following the inevitable stages of atrophy and content
dilution. These entrepreneurs got more this period than
they had bargained for; Afro-American models developed
the intense-swinging, -driving approach, one of the multitude of inimitable approaches garnered from Jazz of the
past and Afro-American church music.

With the advent of this new music, bop, the creative
energy hitherto invested in the production of dance music
was transferred to the performer. And although the dance
function was still evident in the bop and jitterbug dances,
the role of dancer became secondary to that of listener.
Whereas before, the music had been heard, it now required concentrated listening, allowing an expansion of
self through identification with the symbolic communication of the performer. (There are conceptual differences
between hearing and listening. The former includes other
stimuli besides music, and can be an accompaniment to
other activities. Listening requires concentration, restrict-
ing itself to only aural musical stimuli.) The performer,
in turn, was for the first time in the position of practically
unlimited self-expression, no longer confined to the role
of providing a dance beat. Previously an uncomplicated,
clearly accented beat had facilitated complicated rhythms
and improvisation in the dance, but now the process became focused on the music as a primary function in itself.
The beat could become more complex and stimulate the
soloist to new improvisatory feats. The rhythm section,
rather than audience-dancer reaction, "fed" the soloist.
What appeared to be performer indifference during this
period was the result of concentration mainly on artistic
rapport, communicational inputs could now flow from

* "The Loneliest Monk," *Time* magazine, June 1964, p. 86.

player to player in a musical system which contained its own feedback devices.

Sweeping aside external pretensions, bop revived that which was individual, internal and essential in music. The introspective domains of man, as expressed in Afro-American music, had by then given way almost completely to requirements of mass popularity, a popularity shaped by an increasingly centralized industry. With the exception of the Blues and some of the compositions of composers such as Duke Ellington and Fletcher Henderson, much of the music had been geared to the external appeals of box-office receipts, Tin Pan Alley royalties and radio contracts. Technical innovations in recordings had severed the intimate and interdependent connections between performers and audience, the mainstay of New Orleans Jazz and Ragtime. Machines replaced the artist, and the artist lost control over his products. Centralization of the music industry led to mass migrations of musicians from local areas to New York and Chicago. Respect for the local musician diminished as popularity of the music industry's national radio or recording artists increased.

The money men did not realize the value and influence of these "local" players. Zito Carno tells of hearing John Coltrane playing two and three notes at once, "not that little trick some reedmen use of humming or singing a note and playing another, but honest to goodness notes. . . . That was when I found out about harmonics on a tenor saxophone. 'Trane told me he'd learned how to do them from some tenor man in Philly, who had been working on them for some time, and 'only now I'm starting to get them.'" * (Author's emphasis)

Coleman Hawkins, in an interview with Nat Hentoff, gave credit to local musicians for introducing the tenor saxophone to Jazz †:

---

* Zito Carno, John Coltrane—Coltrane Jazz—Atlantic Records.

† To the extent that all Jazz musicians originally came from a distinct locale, all have been local at one time or another.

. . . one thing I'd like to clear up. People always say I invented the jazz tenor, that I was the first who played jazz on tenor. It isn't true. There was Happy Cauldwell in Chicago and Stomp Evans out of Kansas City. They were playing like mad.*

The bebop musician was often the subject of jokes and stories during the early stages of the movement. (One of the functions of the joke is to conceal or mask fear and anxiety over an otherwise socially taboo subject.) One of the frequent themes of these jokes was "way out" Jazz musicians perched on "cloud 9" smoking reefer. This supposed obliviousness to reality was reinforced by the usage of bop-derived terms such as *crazy, cool, swinging, cat,* and *dig,* which, when taken out of cultured context, came to connote meanings other than those intended by the musicians. *Dig* had meant to look beneath the surface, uncover the esoteric rather than rely solely on external appearance. Words like *crazy* were a subtle challenge to the conviction that rationality, logic and conventional morality, the backdrops of apparent sanity, were indeed the ultimate standard. *Crazy* was conceptualized as a complimentary adjective rather than a put-down. The term was not diagnostic or clinical, but connoted clarity and profundity of vision. It was a cryptic term of acceptance, intimating a sense of understanding, professional fraternity and appreciation of performance skills. In the hands of the jokesters, *crazy,* like other bop terms, came to have confused implications, relegating the value changes that were taking place to the realm of the absurd.

Soon after whites from upper middle-class families began to imitate the new sounds and behavior, the jokes became sour and the punch lines turned into narcotics arrests. The artistic underground was spreading to the disillusioned sector of society, the sons and daughters of prominent families, who welcomed the new, refreshing culture. Herein we see the precursor of the present-day "hippie," the "beat" generation.

* "The Hawk Talks," *Down Beat* magazine, November 14, 1956, p. 13.

Certainly, the invention of heroin cannot be attributed to Jazz or, more specifically, to bop musicians. The same holds true for its manufacture and distribution. Nor, one can be sure, were a few black bebop artists the only members of society who sometimes partook of the drug between the early Forties and mid-Fifties. Yet to judge by the number of arrests, convictions and widespread publicity given to bop musicians for alleged possession of "horse," as it was called, one would conclude that the above statements were true. For practically all of the outstanding players of bop were arrested during this period, some, like Sonny Rollins and Gene Ammons, receiving long jail terms. When narcotics could not be found, they were either planted by policemen or other charges were preferred. For example, Miles Davis was incarcerated for nonsupport, having to serve over a year's time at the notorious Sing Sing prison in New York. Billie Holiday, though not a part of the bop movement, was hounded from one city to the next, detectives even breaking down her hotel-room door during a Philadelphia engagement in the early Fifties. Detectives somehow always managed to find what they were looking for in such operations, and the media, particularly newspapers and magazines, embellished the stories with morbid details. However, one circumstance that the media never discussed was the wholesale dissemination of opiates into black communities during and following World War Two, the Korean War and the present war in Vietnam.

Now that the white middle-class addicts are greatly increasing in number, a great humanitarian concern is being shown by many of the same authorities who made life miserable for the black bop musician. The terminology has conveniently changed from *dope fiend* and *junkie* to *acid head* and *user of mind-expanding drugs*. It also might come as a surprise to some that during the bop period, and since, an array of symphony conductors and "classical" musicians have been the users of "hard" drugs, especially cocaine. They, however, were not, in society's eyes, musical outlaws. They maintained the society's val-

ues. Their reward from society was immunity from pun-
ishment for their legal transgressions. One conductor,
who shall remain anonymous, could not, for reasons
that became clear later, begin his Sunday afternoon
concert at Tanglewood. Just before the concert, he
drooped into the green room, head bowed, a look of
agony on his face. The general manager seemed furious
at the delay and intent on hiding the spectacle from general purview. A few minutes later, an expensive car sped
from the main entrance to the stage door. Out came a
dignified-looking man carrying a little black bag, the type
that doctors use. He immediately went to the green room
and in a few seconds out came the maestro, this time full
of zest and with smiling countenance. The concert went
splendidly, with the conductor's arms thrashing wildly as
he beat the tempo up to a frenzy. We in the orchestra
knew that he had gotten his fix.

The point is that for bebop musicians a blatant form
of *cultural suppression* was taking place, a suppression
not restricted solely to black musicians, since white bop
players such as Art Pepper and Stan Getz were also arrested for narcotics violations.

Like Ragtime, bebop was a system which could absorb
and transform other musical genre. While Ragtime transformations occurred through syncopated rhythmic structure, bebop not only thoroughly enhanced the latter but
succeeded in a distillation of harmonic structure from
American popular standards with a highly original, individualized treatment of melody. By systematic alteration,
substitution and extension of chord structure to standards
like "I Got Rhythm," or "How High the Moon," infinite
melodic permutations could be composed. This was true
both for the initial melodic statement, or "head," as well
as subsequent solo choruses.

> Be-Bop is especially the intransigent opponent of Tin
> Pan Alley. Indeed the war against the horrible products
> of the tunesmiths, which began . . . in the 1920's, has
> been brought to a successful conclusion only by the
> beboppers, who take standard melodies at will, stand

them on their heads, and create new compositions retaining only a harmonic relationship with the original.
Thus, "What is This Thing Called Love?" becomes "Hot
House"; "How High the Moon" is "Ornithology," and
so on.*

For the first time, black musicians were in the position
to turn the game around and use "white" elements of that
which had been originally borrowed from black culture.
Isaac Goldberg traces the Afro-American's influence on
American music culture leading to Tin Pan Alley:

> Before the various types of jazz was the modern coon
> song; before the coon song was the minstrel show; be-
> fore the minstrel show was the plantation melody and
> the spiritual. It is safe to say that without the Negro we
> should have had no Tin Pan Alley. †

Through the use of ingenious coding techniques having
evolved from New Orleans "head arrangements," entire
songs could be reduced to a few inches of space, with
only chord symbols and the melody or head. This format
largely replaced the customary "long hand" sheet music,
or written-out arrangements, which had evolved from the
days of the big bands. For the white bands, arrangements
had been a necessity on two counts. First, reading from
arrangements precluded the need for improvisation, an
artistic mode virtually intrinsic to Afro-American music
culture. Second, elaborate, expensive arrangements resulted in white competitors gaining ascendancy in the
industry during the Twenties. They were combined with
large personnel, elaborate costumes and music stands,
managers, band boys and valets, the effect of which was
to seriously disadvantage Afro-American musicians without the financial wherewithal to compete against such
"show biz" models. In New York during this era a successful Afro-American orchestra on the order of Vincent
Lopez or Paul Whiteman was an exception.

---

* Martin Williams, editor, *The Story of Jazz* (New York: Oxford University Press, 1959), p. 202.
† Isaac Goldberg, *Tin Pan Alley* (New York: John Day, 1930), p. 32.

The advantage accorded by the shorthand code system so frequently employed during the bop era was the creation of a musical language that could be understood by both those who could read music as well as those who played by "ear." Although piano music had employed chord symbols before, they had been intended mainly for guitar, and were spread over a considerably greater space. Each measure with its appropriate chord symbols contained not only the melody, but harmony and written-out bass and lyrics. Instead of having to use the somewhat unwieldy sheet music version of a composition, two basic types of coding systems were employed. The first example, "Dig," contains both melody and chords.* The second example is a further abbreviated version, employing only chord symbols and beats. In the last format, particularly applicable to piano and bass players, beats are associated with appropriate chords, so that melody, harmony and rhythm are in alignment. In both examples, selection of the five fundamental types of chords—seventh, major, minor, augmented and diminished—is indicated in abbreviated fashion above the root note: maj. 7 min. aug. and dim.

Inasmuch as "standards" (those compositions having greatest popularity during a particular era) were required knowledge of the professional Jazz musician, it was an easy step to their modified usage in the bop aggregation. This situation allowed for a maximum interchange of players, as in the days of New Orleans Jazz. Jazz players could now, more or less, with a minimum of encumbrance, base their performance on a common store of already available material.

Unlike the so-called swing era, when Jazz had been an adjunct to the dance and therefore required the continuous pulsation of the bass drum and guitar, bop was solo-oriented. For this reason, standards chosen for bop composition contained, as a rule, fewer chord changes per measure, allowing a greater space for melodic invention

* "Dig" is a composition by Miles Davis based on the harmonic structure of "Sweet Georgia Brown."

and heightened possibilities for harmonic alteration and substitution.

The drums and guitar, no longer confined to a strict rhythmic function, swiftly evolved into melodic instruments, with the basic impulse or beat shifting from the bass drum to the shimmering, lighter-sounding cymbal. Off-beat syncopation, or "bombs," replaced the previous steady 4/4 beat of the bass drum, increasing musical feed-back (by making the musical structure more elastic) and providing inspiration to the soloist. The "elasticized" mu-sical universe gave more and more varied perspectives from which to begin and provided more varied paths along which to travel for both soloist and rhythm section.

The African concept of drums involving both rhythm and melody was being reasserted more than a hundred years after its banishment during slavery. Art Blakey studied drums in Africa. Dizzy Gillespie employed the Afro-Cuban drummer Chano Pozo in one of his early 1940 bands. As in the days of slavery, some white listeners began to express fears over the verbal-like qualities reasserting themselves. Some, for example, saw bop drumming as indicative of hate, and portending revolution and violence.

Bass players were also to gain a new measure of freedom now that the rhythm guitar had evolved into a melodic instrument. With fewer but more complex chords to work with, and independence from the rhythm guitar concept, bass players could now concentrate on lines of a contra-puntal character and fittingly complement those of the soloist. Instead of the routine root to fifth movements, additional space was available for passing and other non-chordal tones. The entire range of the bass, along with the other instruments used in the bop era, was opened to experimentation. "Walking," another word with aural-physical association, was the term used to characterize the even, measured flow of the bass line, providing both harmonic outline and rhythmic impulse.

The final component of the bop rhythm section was the piano. Following the Ragtime era, the piano had for the most part been conceived as a solo instrument, but now its role, as well as those of other members of the rhythm sec-tion, was radically altered. With bop, the big-band format of multiples of the same instrument was altered. There was a reduction in instrumentation. The trio, quartet or quintet became the basic unit. Correspondingly, each instrument in the reduced unit's rhythm section was given more responsibilities and roles, encompassing both accompaniment and solo functions. As a solo instrument, the piano formerly had required extensive use of the left hand in order to fill in the bass line. Now that this function was undertaken by the bass player, the bop pianist was in a position to concentrate on and develop the technique of the right hand for solo playing and both hands for expansive harmonic statements. A constant bass line supplying chordal structure allowed greater space and more time for preparation of unusual harmonic substitutes and extensions. When not soloing, the bop pianist, rather than fill in every beat, "comped" or provided vertical tonal aggregates, from which the line men or soloists could draw melodic statements. The seeds were being sown for the percussive pianistic quality which is so evident in the styles of contemporary Jazz pianists.

Bop was a major challenge to European standards of musical excellence and the beginning of a conscious black aesthetic in music. Since the Twenties, when the term "sweet" was created to imply that a new style had arisen among the white imitators of New Orleans Jazz, a sort of orthodoxy had become manifest in terms of tone production. "Sweet" came to describe, not an innovation in content or style, but tonal production that was characterized by a wide vibrato. Although vibrato had been employed in African and Afro-American music for expressive effect or nuance, under the European-influenced imitators in the Twenties, it had been used continuously, in accordance with traditional European canons of style. Therein, tone without continuous vibrato was considered to be indicative of inferior playing. As with other "new" periods of Afro-American music, the originators were forced, out of commercial necessity, to imitate their imitators. The latter, by inculcating such European aesthetic criteria, were then able to give the appearance of innovation and thus force commercial models on black musicians.

Shock waves throughout the industry were felt with the advent of vibrato-less tones in the Forties. The iconoclastic figures of Lester Young, Charlie Parker, Dizzy Gillespie and Miles Davis suddenly altered the European conception by tonal production that was unarguably beautiful, even though based on non-European standards. European criteria of tonal quality are to a great extent based upon speed or frequency of continuous vibrato within a carefully circumscribed range. Vibrato that is "too fast" or "too slow" is judged as productive of "bad" tone. Vibrato in Afro-American music has not been subjected to this degree of stylization, being dependent on expressive mood and therefore capable of greater variation in terms of speed or frequency.

Other serious challenges to the uniform European aesthetic concerned the outcropping of personalized methods of playing. Breaking away from European notions of the "correct" way to play, men like Gillespie experimented with methods that had heretofore been considered wrong. The puffed cheeks of Gillespie defied notions that the diaphragm must be the sole source of air production. Later he was to turn the bell of his trumpet from the accustomed horizontal position to a sixty-degree angle. Babs Gonzales wrote, sang and recorded bop compositions such as "Oop-Pop-A-Da" which replaced conventional lyrics with those of his own invention. Commenting on the music industry's tendency to credit whites with black developments, Gonzales remarked: "Charlie Ventura was the first to emulate our style and in two months of constant plugging by this snake (a radio disc jockey) *he* became the ORIGINATOR of the bop vocals." * (Author's emphasis)

Finally, even though European music had employed dissonance, it was conventional and prescribed that a composition end on a consonance. Bop pieces, however, frequently defied this rule by ending on dissonances.

With the sudden barrage of innovations and deviations

* Babs Gonzales, *I Paid My Dues* (New York: Lancer Books, 1967), p. 45.

from European musical norms, would-be white imitators were, as never before or since, thrown off the path to easy accessibility.

The total effect of this barrage was that Afro-American musicians gained a measure of control over their product, a situation that had not existed since the expansion of the music industry in the Twenties. Even though whites still controlled radio and the phonograph industry, they could no longer dominate the performance field. The constant drive of the bop rhythm section, coupled with an inscrutable Afro-American ethos in soloistic playing, sharply delimited white competition. If one compares the recordings of whites with those of black players, musical differences are immediately recognizable. Leonard Bernstein and other non-Blacks "interested" in Afro-American culture must have sighed a breath of relief when, in the late Fifties, new, less artistically demanding models were found. Bernstein had stated in a widely quoted article that Ornette Coleman was to be the next major influence in Jazz, and almost overnight many Afro-American musicians were talking about bop as being old-fashioned as they hurried to alter their styles to conform to the new, media-created expectations. Here are the words of Langston Hughes:

"It may be gone, but its riffs remain behind," said Simple! Bebop music was certainly colored folks' music —which is why white folks found it so hard to imitate. But there are some few white boys that latched onto it right well. And no wonder, because they sat and listened to Dizzy, Thelonius, Tad Dameron, Charlie Parker, also Mary Lou, all night long every time they got a chance, and bought their records by the dozen to copy their riffs. The ones that sing tried to make up new bebop words, but them white folks don't know what they are singing about, even yet.*

* Langston Hughes, "Bop," from *Tales of Simple* in *Black Voices*, edited by Abraham Chapman (New York: New American Library, 1968), p. 104.

8

The Contemporary Era

> Look what they've done to my song, ma
> Look what they've done to my song
> (As sung by Ray Charles)

Traveling northward from Philadelphia on the Penn Central one arrives at Trenton, New Jersey, and is greeted by a singular sign: TRENTON MAKES—THE WORLD TAKES. This greeting to New Jersey's capital ironically could be a slogan of the black musician: I MAKE—THE WORLD TAKES. The city of Trenton makes the announcement with pride, for in actuality the sign means TRENTON MAKES—THE WORLD BUYS, and Trenton is a beneficiary of the purchase. The black musician can make the boast with little pride. The slogan for him in actuality means I MAKE—THE WORLD BUYS . . . FROM WHITE MUSICIANS.

White musicians in the Jazz rock fields are derivative and ancillary to the production of black music gaining their stature by the completeness of their imitation of Afro-American source models. In order for the process to take place with maximal efficiency and to avoid the confusion involved in discrimination of highly variable stimuli, only a comparatively few black source models are chosen at any one point in time. Preferably they contain as little variation as possible, for quick assimilation and subsequent duplication. And, perhaps most important for our discussion, the chosen models contain a minimum of elements intrinsic to Afro-American culture, since these cannot be copied easily and are therefore useless to the industry, regardless of ther aesthetic value. One such element almost absent in today's Jazz but clearly an integral part of the Jazz of the Forties and Fifties was swing, hard swing. Few white musicians could really feel comfortable with bop; thus the money men sought new models. The critics and Jazz writers continuously assailed those Afro-American players who swung hard and who placed emphasis on emotive expression.

The atmosphere during the Forties and Fifties contained all the ingredients of an inquisition, with implicit warnings to those who refused to temper their playing. Common were epithets such as "hostile," "naked emotionalism," "angry," "fiery," "explosive," and "hate-inspired." John Coltrane's playing was described as sheets of sound and *mere* scales by Ira Gitler. To others it was too emotive, and therefore suggestive to whites of hate and violence. Speaking of Sonny Rollins's return from retirement, one critic observed that "what had once sounded like music from hate, seemed now to come out from love." *

Accordingly, critics and writers launched campaigns to explain the reasons for this hypothesized anger, the black man's pride in his art and his belief that the ascendant positions in the field, financially and otherwise, belonged to him.

> It is because Negroes are denied full acceptance outside jazz that they take such fierce pride in the fact that at least jazz is theirs, that it began as Afro-American music, and that the majority of its most internationally applauded figures are Negro. †

In other words, pride in Jazz can be reduced to a *reaction* against something, rather than a positive artistic

* John S. Wilson, *Jazz: The Transition Years* (New York: Appleton-Century-Crofts, 1966), p. 61.

† Nat Hentoff, *The Jazz Life* (New York: Dial Press, 1961), pp. 65-66.

accomplishment that affirms and confirms Afro-American culture. Followed to its logical conclusion, pride in Afro-American music, and the music itself, would cease to exist once barriers to other musical employment were dropped.

This black music was too hot to handle and musicians such as Shorty Rogers, Chet Baker, Dave Brubeck and Gerry Mulligan latched onto "cooler" source models such as Lester Young, Miles Davis and Ben Webster. They attempted to formulate a musical recipe that would in effect sidestep the otherwise inaccessible regions of Afro-American musical culture—a music in which hard-driving swing (hot) could be replaced by inertia (cool). Such a movement was bound to fail since it confused the apparent detachment of the above source models with coolness, producing a lackluster music whose novelty effect was short-lived. The Cool School referred to a state of intellectualism which preempted all other performance considerations. Neshui Ertegun explains that the Cool School sought "order, clarity, continuity, structure, rather than uncontrolled outbursts and wild exhibitionism. The influence of classical music is naturally very strong." *

Following the "cool" school there was yet another move toward Europe—the so-called third stream. Third stream represented nothing new in terms of inculcating Afro-American music culture into European classical works. Debussy, Ravel, Satie, Milhaud, Ives and Stravinsky had done so at earlier periods. Again it was merely the process of labeling and relabeling of the same concept for the purposes of stimulating lagging consumer interests.

The "West Coast" and "cool" schools had by the mid-Fifties become so frozen that emotion was lacking altogether, a state of affairs that held little appeal for even white audiences. Musical atrophy and dilution had once again set in. Another cultural escape hatch was required to bail out white musicians from the dilemma of not being able to play so-called "funk and soul," the commercial label

* Neshui Ertegun, "Modern Jazz," *The Record Changer,* Summer, 1954, p. 18.

for music emanating from the Afro-American spirit and culture at that time.

Third stream rested upon the proposition, so frequently stated by white critics and musicologists, that Afro-American music and specifically Jazz was an amalgam of European elements superimposed on an African base. (We could expect, if this formulation were correct, that European classical musicians would find as little difficulty playing Jazz as Afro-American musicians find in playing classical music. Furthermore, we would predict that Jazz would develop along similar lines to European classical and that historically there would be as many outstanding white players and true source models as Afro-American. Since none of the above predictions hold forth in the real world, we may conclude that such formulations are not grounded empirically but mere supposition.) Although this formulation has never been demonstrated, it nonetheless provided a theoretical framework by which third stream, the combination of Jazz and Western classical music, could be attempted.

It is in the nature of the music industry that trends are a blessing to some and a bane to others. They assist the industry in regulating popular demand and the setting and manipulation of taste. It is highly favorable to the industry to have as few trends present at any one time or period to avoid confusion in consumer discrimination.

Although the third-stream movement was advocated by some Afro-American musicians, white interest groups were mainly being served. For some black musicians, trapped in a seemingly endless cycle of low pay, dingy night clubs and lack of respect as artists, third stream meant a possible deliverance to the higher paying, more respectful and rarefied world provided for European classical musicians by the wielders of cultural power.

For the symphony, third stream promised a new lease on life, a shot in the arm to a moribund institution. The attempted transplantation of European cultural forms and vehicles of expression was disintegrating on alien soil. The symphony held less and less appeal for the young white audience which had traditionally succeeded older generations at the concert hall. Older white American audiences had attended symphony concerts more for social ritual than for aesthetic pleasure, providing a complementary audience structure for a severely attenuated repertoire, mechanistic standardization and chilling predictability. The only symphony orchestra in America that has consistently maintained full houses is that of Boston, undoubtedly because of the city's symbolic position as the "seat" of Anglo-Protestant culture. A large percentage of its membership is, however, not of WASP but European immigrant descent, who have become "naturalized" Americans.

> The deterministic role of the conductor has been grossly exaggerated—as have the roles of all leaders, political and social. Regardless of who wields the "authority" there is a basic repertoire, often referred to facetiously as the "standard fifty pieces," which is not fiction but reality. . . . The easy interchange of conductors between distant orchestras even internationally is both evidence and a product of this standardization of musical "parts." . . . A large proportion of an audience actually desires a program a little above its heads. To such listeners the symphony concert is more than mere musical delight; it is ritual and ceremony of which all the social trappings and even the intellectual affectations are a part. To many patrons, concerts are a fashion in which prestige of participation takes priority over spontaneous aesthetic relaxation.*

To judge from events between the mid-Fifties and the present, the implicit marriage between symphony and Jazz has turned out sour and predicated upon European chauvinism. For although it is true that more and more whites have been given entry to Afro-American music, the converse has not occurred, for there is still today only

* John H. Mueller, *The American Symphony Orchestra* (Bloomington, Indiana: Indiana University Press, 1951), pp. 398–399.

a token handful of Afro-Americans employed in symphonies. Likewise, when third-stream concerts take place,
either involving small or large (symphony) groups, they
inevitably involve a substantially greater percentage of
white musicians than Afro-American. Arthur Fiedler,
sometimes described as the conductor of "middle America," gave a television presentation on July 25, 1971,
featuring, with one exception, an all-white Boston "Pops"
orchestra along with Gerry Mulligan, Dave Brubeck, Paul
Desmond and one Afro-American who was not featured,
drummer Alan Dawson. When Jazz compositions written
by white musicians are scored solely for orchestra and do
not call for a Jazz support group, there are likely to be no
Afro-American performers. Such a situation took place
during the Fifties when a jazz composition by Rolf Liber-
man was premiered by the Chicago Symphony, an organization that has steadfastly refused to even in some cases
honor applications by Afro-Americans, let alone to employ a single Afro-American musician in its entire eighty-
one years of existence.*

As the stage shifted from utilization of ethnic source
materials, e.g., "funk-soul," to attempts to combine Western classical and Jazz, criteria of evaluation were set into
motion almost exclusively based upon the premises gov-
erning European aesthetics: technical prowess, complexity and formalism. Though this tendency had been latent
on occasion from the onset of Jazz criticism, it now could
manifest itself openly and with regularity. Resolution of
the inevitable conflicts between the two opposing aesthetics and correlative issues involving phrasing, reading,
spontaneity and creative license were resolved for the
most part by a compromise of Afro-American aesthetic
requirements.

  The joint Town Hall concert (1959) by the Modern
  Jazz Quartet and the Beaux Arts, one of the country's

* The Ford Foundation's Humanities and Arts Program in 1968
awarded $2 million in matching grants and $400,000 in nonmatching endowments to the Chicago Symphony.

best string quartets, involved a new work each by John Lewis and Gunther Schuller. It also involved one's early apprehension about just what kind of music that was going to be. The best way to begin is on the more familiar ground of what each group did separately.

A lovely performance of Haydn Opus 74, No. 1 by the Beaux Arts Quartet could teach us a lot. We do a lot of talking about group integration and responsiveness; these men live by it, musically and visually. We also talk about jazz as the "living" music; this music is as alive to these men as anything the MJQ plays is to its members. There has been a lot of talk since the twenties about classicists having cut themselves off from the dance. Not only in the minuet but throughout this piece, these men were more directly in touch with dancing than half of the jazzmen, including mainstreamers, now playing in New York. And the complexity of texture that four instruments achieve in their idiom should be a challenge to everybody. . . .

Everyone said that John Lewis' "Sketch" was well titled: actually it was barely a sketch and just a bit more than a trifle. But a very successful trifle and based on the same kind of eloquently simple melody that his best pieces have. It demonstrated something perhaps learned in that unfortunate encounter with the Stuttgart Orchestra last year, as if Lewis had said, "Very well, these men phrase differently. Can I write a piece in which I do not try to make them accent our way, but let *them use their idiom while we use ours, and still maintain unity?*" The answer seems to be that he could, at least with a sketch.*

Obviously the implication is that John Lewis had to modify his work to accommodate an alien aesthetic, but the piece nonetheless enhanced the box-office appeal of a European orchestra. It, like its American counterparts, has never been known to allow such compromise or liberties when concerned with European performance re-

* Martin Williams, editor, *Jazz Panorama* (New York: Dial, 1964), p. 301.

quirements of Afro-American auditionees or token members of symphonies. Likewise, Afro-American auditionees are never judged by how well they perform compositions containing explicit Afro-American idioms. Compositions for auditions are chosen from the "standard fifty."

By the early Sixties, the third stream had become a trickle of effete-sounding Jazz! Quiet and sedate, but devoid of outward or inward emotion.

With the reification of third-stream music and the resulting tendency to evaluate Afro-American music according to Western values and aesthetics, it was predictable that future white, as well as black, players would be judged more in accordance with European rather than Afro-American standards. This compromising of Afro-American aesthetics also made possible a greater number of white performers who could with more assurance be safely judged by white critics as outstanding.

And lastly, the emphasis on desegregation (an aftermath of the 1954 Supreme Court decision forbidding segregated schools) resulted indirectly in the formation of amalgamated musicians' unions. The loss of institutional support and control vested in Afro-American locals led to a diffusion of black musicians into white musicians' unions, removing their former identity as a special interest group. Work within black communities formerly under the jurisdiction of separate locals decreased after coming under the control of the forces which had previously excluded Afro-Americans from higher paying jobs in symphony, opera, theater, etc. Before amalgamation, the black musician was told: You are different from us (whites) and must join a Negro local. With amalgamation, the formulation changed to: You are no different from us, so don't pull that "Black stuff" on us. What remained constant? You black musicians are still unqualified to play our best-paying jobs: symphony, opera, society, theaters, etc. But if you want to play Jazz, you had better integrate *your* units.*

* For a more detailed account and analysis of union amalgamation see pp. 162–166.

Third-stream novelties played a more important role
in contemporary Jazz than is generally conceded. Not
only can the third-stream development be seen in terms
of Western value orientations as applied to Afro-American
music, but also in its effect upon professional careers of
certain white musicians. Third stream provided an al-
ternative to the culturally impossible route of creativity
based primarily upon Afro-American cultural sources.
Bill Evans, who had in the earlier days imitated "Bud"
Powell, was unable to develop into a creative pianist
without the aid of third stream. Dizzy Gillespie could develop creatively after following the model of Roy Eldridge
because of his continuous and not ad hoc existence within
the culture of Afro-America. Thus the Afro-American
musician who hears and identifies with models from his
culture has potentially within himself the seeds of individuality grounded in Afro-American culture. The white
player, by definition, no matter how politically liberal or
well versed in Afro-American cultural lore, is beholden
to a life experience based primarily upon European cultural tenets which subsequently hinder artistic sensibility
within Afro-American realms. His life experience within
a country that *does* place emphasis on color, despite egalitarian notions of color blindness, precludes all but a part-
time existence in the context of black experience and
culture. Scott LaFaro, Evans's bassist, dismisses the roots
and traditions of Jazz in an interview with Martin Williams:

> I first heard Percy Heath and Paul Chambers on the
> juke box. They taught me my first jazz bass lessons. I
> found out playing with Bill that I have a deep respect
> for harmony, melodic patterns, and form . . . I can't
> abandon them. That's why I don't think that I could
> play with Ornette Coleman. I respect the way he over-
> rides forms. It's all right for him, but I don't think
> I could do it myself. Bill gives the bass harmonic free-
> dom because of the way he voices, and he is practically
> the only pianist who does. It's because of his classical
> studies. Many drummers know too little rhythmically,

and many pianists know too little harmonically. I don't like to look back, because the whole point in jazz is doing it now. My main problem now is to get that instrument under my fingers so I can play more music.*

According to Williams, a few weeks after the foregoing interview LaFaro did become a member of the Ornette Coleman quartet for several engagements. In the process, he gained enough prestige to allow for the dissemination of technically oriented novelties. Afro-American bassists came under considerable pressure to imitate the imitator. This meant an aesthetic compromise, the relinquishment of the vital force of Jazz, its physics, pulsation and rhythmicity, for rapidity of technical display.

Third-stream music caused considerable anxiety among older black musicians. The experience of being a dedicated Afro-American Jazz musician who has spent the many years of practice necessary to the attainment of mastery of Afro-American classical music (Jazz) can easily lead to frustration when events are brought about which threaten his career and occupational mobility. Unlike European classical music, with its seemingly boundless sources of public and institutional support, Afro-American classical music is almost completely dependent on the dictates of an industry controlled by non-black ethnic groups. The industry's appeal has been to the young, those having the greatest interest in peer-group recognition that accrues from following the latest fashions, or trends.

For this reason, age-linked expectations severely impinge on the careers of most Afro-American Jazz musicians. With few exceptions, Jazz careers tend to decline after the performer reaches the age of thirty.

The typical career sequence of a Jazz musician involves a relatively long apprenticeship phase, largely consisting of physically exhausting road work, after which there is a brief time span remaining for artistic consolidation and career promotion, in which the artist is either "made"

* *Op. cit.*, pp. 278–280.

or broken. Many of those who are selected and "made" by the industry die in the exhausting scramble to achieve fame and relative financial security, before the age of forty. The late Lee Morgan (a recent victim of premature death) includes those over forty in his discussion of the above career contingencies:

> I think one of the main reasons why Louis died . . . I saw him on his last engagement in New York, and he had to lay down between shows. The man had just had a heart attack; he shouldn't have been playing. This is the tragedy of the Black artist: just to live halfway comfortably he must keep on working! That's not to say they don't have *any* money—I'm talking about in perspective to their talent. These people should have shrines dedicated to them, just like they have shrines in Europe to Beethoven and Bach; Louis Armstrong especially and Duke Ellington as well.*

During the interval between the onset of the Jazz career and its attenuation, there is little time for the development of alternate career roles. With these considerable sacrifices in mind, the sudden, widely hailed emergence of *anyone* deviating from previously defined artistic limits raises considerable anxiety in those who have painstakingly attempted continuous artistic modification in order to conform to subjective critical evaluations. Ornette Coleman and his approach caused considerable discussion:

> "I listened to him all kinds of ways," Roy Eldridge told a friend. . . . "I even played with him. I think he's jiving, baby. He's putting everybody on. They start with a nice lead-off figure, but then they go off into outer space. They disregard the chords and they play odd numbers of bars. I can't follow them. I even listened to him with Paul Chambers, Miles Davis' bass player. 'You're younger than me,' I said to him. 'Can you follow Ornette?' Paul said he couldn't either. . . ." †

---

* "Lee Morgan, The Last Interview," by Mike Bourne, *Down Beat* magazine, April 27, 1972.
† Nat Hentoff, *The Jazz Life* (New York: Dial, 1961), p. 228.

"Red" Garland, Miles Davis's pianist at the time, expressed similar attitudes toward Coleman's playing:

> Nothing's happening. I wouldn't mind if he were serious. I like to see a struggling cat get a break. But Coleman is faking. . . . What surprises me is that he fooled someone like John Lewis.*

It is not surprising that Louis Armstrong took a similar position in the late Forties, generalized to an entire school of Jazz, bebop.

These pressures away from conformity and/or conservatism would be considered regenerative and representative of a healthy artistic diversity if they were operating within the European classical field. But in the Afro-American classical field these deviations are interpreted as the first sign fulfilling the fear of inevitable career displacement. The musicians feel that there is little room for diversity.

Tradition and the Jazz Critic

In the view of most contemporary historian-analysts of music, it seems Jazz is divisible into ten-year periods, as though discrete segments could be neatly chopped off to display what is seen as new or distinctive and thus representative of the decade under discussion. Such a procedure implies that the most recent of Afro-American music is a totally unique, thus unstable phenomenon, rather than part of a continuum of cultural expression. Compare the relatively long time periods between eras of European classical music, where units of one hundred years or more are employed, along with the familiar enjoinder that long periods of historical-aesthetic hindsight are required before valid judgment can be made on certain European classical works that deviate from the norm. Also, this short-run procedure tends to separate that portion of the music selected by the music industry to be sold and marketed as "THE NEWEST HIPPEST THING," from

* *Ibid.*, p. 229.

its ongoing totality and spiritual base. This base and totality are independent of and exist beyond the created momentary fads cultivated so assiduously by the record and television cartels. The vast majority of Afro-American musical creators, the so-called local musicians (those who do not achieve national prominence), are never heard by the mass public, since the commercial demand for mainly white imitators may be increased by conscious regulation of supply. Of course, the audience in actuality has minimal control in terms of what it receives. It can take only what has been made available, much as with any other marketed product. They are, in effect, the subject of endless market experiments; that is, whatever sells best is produced most, and what sells best is the latest fashion, the latest trend. The trends and fads thus created cater to the American market and dictate, for ease of imitation by whites, only a modicum of content variation.

Implications for Afro-American music's being conceptualized as discrete units which cancel each other out in their succession to fashion are:

1. Jazz audiences become age-linked; an association is established between age of audience, player and era of musical content.

2. Breaks with, or denial of, tradition result.

3. Arbitrary norms of value and competency based upon subjective criteria are legitimized by those in control of the product.

4. Validity of previous work is contested or challenged.

The phenomenon is visible in the so-called trends of Afro-American music, especially its classical (Jazz) branch. Whatever was in in 1950, is out in 1960, and whatever is in in 1960 is out in 1970, etc. It goes without saying that what was in in 1910 or 1920 is out forever more.

The role of the Jazz critic (almost always white) is to define, within the structures of the industry, sets of norms concerning aesthetic value and competency based upon reviews of recorded material and, to a lesser degree, live performance.

In some instances the role of critic (definition-maker)

is combined with that of recording-company executive. For example, Ralph Gleason and Leonard Feather act in both capacities. Direct links are then placed between the product and its critical evaluation. Control over content and diversity may then be exercised more fully.

Over the years several measuring instruments of questionable reliability have been devised by Jazz critics to provide an index of value or competency. These include: 1. The magazine poll, a ranking system based allegedly on a cross section of the Jazz public, and 2. A rating system used in the critique of Jazz recordings. In the first system, categories of players (recorded players) can be arranged according to number, the lower the number, the higher the evaluation. The numbers (scores) are presumed to indicate degrees of competency so that comparisons may be made within and between polls. The assumption is that the Jazz-listening audence may be located within the magazine readership, and that the norm is one man, one vote. In point of fact, however, it is possible to stuff the ballot box and to have a population of voters that is not representative. Furthermore, the contestants are not representative of the universe of players since the polls only include recorded players, those who have been groomed or are being groomed as possible musical role-models/source-models.

Among professional attributes, awards constitute ends in themselves, as symbols of work achievement beyond that motivated by self-interest. With few exceptions, the most prestigious awards have been reserved for whites in music and the arts in general. As a recent example, the Grammy Award for Jazz musician of 1972 was given to Bill Evans, passing over two highly creative and proven masters, Miles Davis and Dizzy Gillespie. Ironically, it was Miles Davis who, in the mid-Fifties, gave Evans his first gig with a nationally known group. A recent disclosure indicates that efforts are now underway to establish professional associations among Afro-American Jazz musicians for the purpose of granting awards deemed more in keeping with Afro-American musical values.

Rock: A Case of Misnomer

Acid rock, hard rock, soft rock, country rock, folk rock, psychedelic rock, Jazz rock. Fascinating; like a geological exposition from the latest moon voyage. Sure, far out, but what is this music in reality? When I asked a related question during early 1970 to several hundred professional Jazz musicians, many answered, "Well, it's something that white people invented." A few said that it was something that white people invented "that was like the Blues." With one exception they neglected to see that rock *was* Blues with visual-electronic novelty effects:

> Rock and Roll, the term that later reduced to rock by the Beatles and others, in fact derived from the expression used in Blues of Muddy Waters, who still remains relatively obscure. Coinage of new terms for old things is one of the abilities brought by the Europeans to America, the ability to advertise.*

Miles Davis said, in an interview for *Zygote* magazine in 1970:

> In rock groups the guys know so little about harmonies. It's a shame because they don't study. They deal in visual appearance and loudness, and in sex. . . . All the jazz musicians can play any school of music because they have the knowledge. It's usually the rock musicians that don't have a musical background. They just pick up on something. They just play regular triad kind of sound. †

Without knowledge, and puffed with arrogance, these white musicians (along with the critical establishment) set themselves up as the standard of Blues playing. The problem is not that they play black music but that they become, in the eyes of the larger public, *the* players. Concerning Richie Havens, a black performer who sometimes

* Ishmael Reed, from an interview conducted by the author, February 1970.

† *Zygote* magazine, August 12, 1970, pp. 30–39.

plays and sings imitation white Blues songs, John Lennon made the following comment:

> I think there's a guy called Richard Valens, no, Richie Havens, does he play a very strange guitar? He's a black guy that was on a concert and sang "Strawberry Fields" or something. He plays a pretty funky guitar. *But he doesn't seem to be able to play in the real terms at all.**

The most revealing comment about Afro-American Blues sources came from the famed, and late, Janis Joplin:

> Young white kids have taken the groove and the soul from black people and added intensity. Black music is understated. I like to fill it full of feeling—to grab somebody by the collar and say "Can't you understand me?" Blues is a simple form—anyone can learn it. . . . It's a white concept; they can't have this and they can't have that. Me I was brought up in a white middle class family—I could have anything, but you need something more in your gut, man. †

Now that "rock" has also begun to make its appearance in the "lily white" symphonies (e.g., Chuck Mangione's rock concert and recording with the Rochester Symphony), a process has been set in motion to absorb and assimilate Afro-American music, once and for all.

> Rock, jazz and other pop music seem to be entering a period when their dilution into older dramatic forms and styles—oratorio, cantata, musical, ballet, opera— will gradually take place without arousing fear or disdain from conservatives. That may turn out to be healthier for the older music than for rock and jazz. When popular culture is watered down for the purposes of stabilizing politics or forfending heresies, some of its magnetism and vigor must be diminished. . . . But that should worry only the politicians of pop, for whom art

---

* Jann Wenner, "John Lennon," *Rolling Stone* magazine, January 7, 1971, p. 33.
† "Learning the Saturday Night Swindle," San Francisco *Chronicle*, May 26, 1970, p. 17.

is no more than a weapon, a very blunt one, for beating opponents. More important, we know that the history of significant works that have grown out of vulgar soil can be traced at least as far back as Dufay's 15th century mass, "L'Homme arme." We are not dealing here with some strange new phenomenon but with the systole and diastole of art itself.*

Since Blacks have at present only tangential, if any, control over that which they create and produce, they are in no position to do much about it.

* Donal Henahan, "Where Has the Hunt for Novelty Brought Us?" *The New York Times,* August 15, 1971, p. 11.

9

Arthur Davis, a Suit
Against the New York Philharmonic

> It is shameful for a major cultural institution, one that
> gives concerts in a beautiful new hall financed by public
> subscription, to cling to the color bar while other fields
> are in the process of discarding it. . . . Behind the red
> and gold facade of our major cultural institutions is the
> rotten stench of racism.
> —Whitney M. Young, Jr.
> *The New York Post,* November 7, 1969

The black American musician is in the paradoxical position of, on the one hand, contributing his vast powers to
the creation of a distinctive national and international
music, while on the other hand access is denied to European cultural transplants to America (e.g., symphony orchestras). He is also caught in a predicament in which
whites have an unlimited access to the forms and fruits of
his artistic labors while severe restrictions are placed on
professional entry of Afro-Americans into the citadels of
white European culture.

Jazz is supposedly democratic and free. It is furthermore, according to many of its white critics, the product
of European as well as African influence. Therefore it is
assumed that non-black musicians have a right, perhaps
even a duty, to be gainfully employed in the production
of music related to the black life experience. European
music, however, makes no claims to being either demo-

cratic or free. It is reserved mainly for the white élite who have highly specialized talents and a European cultural background. There are exceptions but these lie for the most part outside the realm of intense social and artistic interaction that takes place among full-time participants in the symphony orchestra setting. A few Afro-American concert singers, a few expatriated conductors, and a single pianist comprise the group of exceptions. They are soloists fulfilling a part-time role in the symphonic group setting, allowed to present themselves to an élite audience which often views them as creatures of natural talent or the products of gifted white music teachers.

Blind Tom is an early example of a black genius viewed in this manner. As a performer of both Afro-American and European classical music, he was treated as datum for scientific examination. His concerts, demonstrating abilities far beyond anything as yet heard, caused his audiences to be baffled and bewildered. The "natural talent" argument was advanced: *

> Seventeen teachers of music in Philadelphia spontaneously testify over their own signatures as follows: "The undersigned find it impossible to account for these immense results upon any hypothesis growing out of the known laws of art and science. In the numerous tests to which Tom was subjected in our presence, or by us, he invariably came off triumphant. Whether in deciding the pitch or component parts of chords the most difficult and dissonant, whether in repeating with correctness and precision any pieces, written or impromptu, played to him for the first and only time, whether in his improvisations of performances of compositions by Thalberg, Gottschalk, Ascher, Verdi, and others—in fact, under every form of musical examination . . . he showed a power and capacity ranking him among the most wonderful phenomena recorded in music history.

* Gunther Schuller, *Early Jazz* (New York: Oxford University Press, 1968), p. 16.

> . . . He is still developing new and startling powers,
> the existence of which have been vouchsafed by the
> *power of God* to Tom alone. (Author's emphasis) *

Euro-Americans found it impossible simply to accept
that Blind Tom could have talent and the ability to play
European music well. Charley Mingus's account of his
experience with a European teacher suggests that this
attitude is manifest in contemporary times:

> When I was learning bass with Rheinschagen he was
> teaching me to play classical music. He said I was close
> but I'd never really get it. So I took some Paul Robeson
> and Marian Anderson records to my next lesson and
> asked him if he thought *those* artists had got it. He said
> they were *Negroes trying* to sing music that was foreign
> to them. [Mingus's emphases] †

The black pianist will be tolerated to a greater extent
than the string player, for there is a status hierarchy related to the playing of various instruments, especially in
the solo category.

One who makes beautiful music on a violin does so
upon an instrument unadorned with mechanical gadgets
and paraphernalia, using an extremely small surface area.
Contrasted with the violin, and other string instruments,
the piano is more limited in the range of tonal subtleties
and modes of tone production. A vibrato is theoretically
impossible on the piano, as are quarter tones and further
subdivisions of the whole tone.

The strings and certain wind instruments, by virtue of
their relative lack of mechanical elaboration, are accorded
higher prestige value, inasmuch as more rigorous requirements attend their mastery. The greatest sense of attainment and prestige is accorded the violinist. Traditionally,
a violinist, the concertmaster, is at the top of the hierarchy

---

* J. A. Rogers, *Africa's Gift to America* (New York: Futuro Press,
1959), p. 231.

† Charles Mingus, *Beneath the Underdog* (New York: Alfred A. Knopf,
1971), pp. 351–352.

of orchestral personnel. He is usually the highest-paid member of the orchestra and sits at its head, nearest the conductor, a position having symbolic significance. Even though black violinists can be traced as far back as the nineteenth century (one of Beethoven's close friends was the black violinist Bridgetower), none have yet been able to extensively concertize or perform solo engagements with American symphony orchestras. The same situation holds true for black viola, cello, double-bass and wind-instrument soloists. Lack of proper training, or of a receptive audience, is the rationale most often advanced by conductor or management.

The critical test of racism in orchestral hiring policy is not in the engagement of a few part-time singers and a pianist. Nor can a decision concerning the absence of racism be based on the employment of only one or two full-time black players. In the latter instances the proportion of white to black players is in the vicinity of 100:1 or 100:2. It would seem that if the standards were of such a nature to exclude most black players, then either the standards should be changed or federal subsidies and tax-exempt foundation grants withdrawn.

With Arthur Davis, a double-bassist, and Earl Madison, a cellist, the lack-of-proper-training rationale could not be used. Mr. Davis had all the proper qualifications and credentials: attendance at the Curtis Institute, one of the nation's most highly rated conservatories, in addition to advanced study at the Manhattan School of Music. Furthermore, he had performed with the Harrisburg (Pennsylvania) Symphony at the age of seventeen, and was bassist with Dizzy Gillespie's band and that of the late John Coltrane. In the Coltrane group he, along with Reggie Workman, developed the concept of two basses, or multiple bass lines, for the Jazz ensemble. Earl Madison graduated with honors from Roosevelt University, and played four years with the Pittsburgh Symphony. Yet after successive auditions with the New York Philharmonic, one of the "big five" of American symphonies, neither was hired for a permanent position. Let us examine some of the circumstances and the outcomes of a case where two blacks sought to enter the higher-paying domains of European music. In this light, the irony of whites having such easy access to the portals of black music will be more clearly seen, and contrasted with the racially discriminatory patterns of American symphony, opera and theater orchestras.

The New York Philharmonic Society, founded in 1824, is the oldest American symphony orchestra. Since that time many orchestras have sprung up in every sizable American city as well as in many smaller cities and towns across the nation.

The first Afro-American to be employed in an American symphony orchestra was Charles Burrell, who was appointed to the Denver Colorado Symphony in 1954. Three years later, the author was appointed to the Boston Symphony, which was the first time a major symphonic orchestra had employed an Afro-American—133 years after the founding of the first such orchestra in America. (A "major" orchestra is one which offers relatively high wages, full-time employment and presumably a high level of artistic accomplishment on the part of the players. There are five major orchestras in this country: the Boston Symphony, Philadelphia Orchestra, Cleveland Symphony, New York Philharmonic and Chicago Symphony.

Most professional symphonies employ an average of one hundred players, with a salary range of several thousand dollars a year for part-time orchestras and a twenty thousand dollars a year average for the major symphonies.* Yearly salaries for orchestras in medium-size cities average aound ten to twelve thousand dollars. First chair, or "principal," players of major orchestras may earn as much as $40,000 per year.

In the "popular" field, of which unfortunately Afro-American classical music, Jazz, is deemed a part, earnings,

---

* "New York Philharmonic musicians are paid a minimum of $305.00 per week, in addition to extra earnings for recordings and television appearances." *The New York Times*, April 11, 1971, p. 19.

except in the cases of a few "stars," are scanty, unpredictable and most often dependent on the wiles of the criminal-syndicate element. The "stars," who make substantial earnings, must also travel, play and record incessantly to arrive and remain on top. An example is B. B. King who, prior to 1969, had not had a vacation in twenty years. Edward Ellington likewise combines an awesome "road" itinerary with his normal schedule of composing and making television guest appearances, in a never-ending cycle.

By 1969, the year that Brothers Davis and Madison brought suit against the New York Philharmonic and Leonard Bernstein, there had been a dramatic 200 percent leap in the number of Afro-Americans engaged in the major orchestras. Now there were two instead of one. This represents about three-tenths of 1 percent of the total (525) men and women thus employed. It is necessary to acknowledge at this point that federal tax dollars, of which black people pay a sizable if not disproportionate share, have been allocated since 1965 to American symphonies. The National Endowment for the Arts and Humanities in 1969 allocated $20 million to symphonies and opera companies. The figure is slated to increase by annual increments of $20 million, so that by 1972, an appropriation of $60 million will be devoted to these causes. In addition, "private" foundations, whose tax-exempt status is made possible by philanthropic grants to nonprofit organizations, provide a sizable contribution to the maintenance of these "European only" cultural establishments.

For Arthur Davis, who had auditioned for the New York Philharmonic on four occasions, and Earl Madison, who had three times auditioned, the outcome could hardly be termed just. The ruling by the New York Commission on Human Rights, after fifteen months of hearings, found the Philharmonic both guilty and not guilty.* The Philharmonic was found not guilty of the main charge of dis-

---

* After consultation with attorneys representing Mr. Madison and Mr. Bernstein, the latter's name was dropped from Mr. Madison's complaint.

crimination against the two black players in terms of permanent hiring. A guilty-of-discrimination verdict was handed down regarding the hiring of substitute and extra players, a procedure which, unlike permanent hiring, did not require auditions.

> The most striking statistic to emerge from the evidence presented was that during the 1960's the respondent [personnel manager Joseph De Angelis] hired at least 277 substitutes or extras who played a total of 1773 weeks during that period. Of these musicians, *one* was black and he played for one week. Interestingly enough, the concerts performed during the week this black musician played included a musical work dedicated to the memories of Dr. Martin Luther King, Jr., and Robert Kennedy. Despite general agreement that this black flutist acquitted himself well, he has not been invited by respondent to return, although white flutists have since been engaged as substitutes.*

Bernstein, who had hosted a gala party for the Black Panthers at his Manhattan penthouse during the course of the case, was seemingly quite annoyed at being subpoenaed before the Commission. On the day that he was summoned from his Connecticut summer home, he was quoted by *The New York Times* (July 31, 1969), in reference to his name being dropped from the list of respondents: "If they don't want to hear from me, why call me here?"

Equally irate sentiments were expressed by several prominent cultural officials at Lincoln Center, the *publicly financed* "home" of the Philharmonic:

> Officials of Lincoln Center and the orchestra have reacted with outrage at being accused of racism. William Schuman, the composer and president emeritus of Lincoln Center, and Leonard Bernstein, the former conductor, have testified that the orchestra's first obligation

---

* Nat Hentoff, "Un-chic Racism at the Philharmonic," *The Village Voice*, December 17, 1970, p. 30.

was to the art and to present the finest musicians available.*

In the music business, things such as reprisals have a
curious way of happening to people who dare to speak
the truth. We have seen what happened to Scott Joplin
when he demanded royalties instead of outright, once-
only payment for his masterpieces. He never sold any
more music, and was unable to successfully stage a production of his opera, *Treemonisha.* This procedure is
aptly enough called blacklisting. Of course, like other
forms of discrimination, particularly those which affect
the individual performer, the charge is difficult to prove,
inasmuch as these actions are covertly accomplished.
Erroll Garner, who had contractual disputes with Columbia Records in the early Sixties, has rarely been heard of
since. Charles Mingus, who dared to vilify in his music
such figures as the former governor of Arkansas, Orville
Faubus, suffered a similar fate. Word somehow gets
around to those non-Blacks who are in charge of the music
industry, and shortly a personal boycott results.

The New York Philharmonic is composed, like other major symphonies, of wealthy and powerful interest groups.
Their concern with the arts may be most often viewed
as supportive to other roles they play in society, politely
masking racism under the facade of culture. This veneer,
in addition to a fanatical devotion to the tenets of Western
European ideas and civilization, assists in the determina-
tion and maintenance of the status quo. When an uppity
"nigger" comes along to test these notions, and to assist
in the redetermination of culture and values, he will then
be punished, forced out of the business.

Such was the case with Arthur Davis and Earl Madison:

> Mr. Davis said that he had recently lost his job with
> the Merv Griffin television show when it moved to the
> West Coast. He said he had regularly been featured on

* Perry Young, "Blacks Say Philharmonic Refuses to Get in Tune," The
New York Post, November 7, 1969, p. 68.

the program, "two or three times a week," but after the hearings began "I was put in my place." Mr. Madison said he was finding it impossible to get recital dates as a result of the case, and was making plans to leave the country. "I have no reason to stay now," he declared.*

In most major symphonies, permanent hiring is based upon two auditions, a preliminary and a final:

> Auditioning procedure calls for preliminary hearings by leading members of the orchestra itself, "although there are no set rules as to who sits in as judges . . . but ultimate responsibility rests with one person," Mr. Mosley said, pointing out that the musical director always presides over the final auditioning. †

The basis for selection in the final audition is loosely termed artistic discretion, and is nominally allocated to the conductor. (Members of the board of trustees, here as with most bureaucracies, wield the power of ultimate decision-making.) Given the fact that neither the preliminary nor the final Philharmonic auditions are held behind a screen (a major point of contention among the complainants), there are possibilities for "margins of error" that might be caused by racism. A player is ostensibly hired for the quality of his playing, not a visual but an aural phenomenon.

Unfortunately, a symphony is very much a visual as well as aural phenomenon, which largely accounts for the dearth of Afro-American players in the first place. Why do symphony orchestras continue to employ the color bar while "other fields are in the process of discarding it"? One answer may lie in the social nature of the orchestra, and the symbolism represented by a large group in the process of intricate, close interaction. Job performance in other occupations which employ Blacks is not, for the

---

* *The New York Times*, November 18, 1970, p. 40. For cynics let me say that it is obvious that the Merv Griffin Show did not move to California in order to deny Arthur Davis employment.

† *Ibid.*, p. 40.

most part, directly involved with public acceptance. Nor do such jobs usually require intricate performance interaction that is publicly viewed. Team sports are an interesting exception; even though color bars have been lifted on a national level, it took years to do so. Baseball did not begin to integrate its ranks until the late Forties with Jackie Robinson. Football and basketball later followed suit.

The question of the use of screens for auditions is highly critical in the case of black auditioners. How does one know that the visual element has not crept into the psychologically complex situation, when Black is judged by white? A conductor or other person charged with the responsibility of choosing among alternate racial possibilities might exercise racism on a subconscious rather than conscious level. He might even harbor racist ideas and sentiments and be a staunch member of a civil rights organization or host a party for the Panthers.

Yet the Philharmonic remained intransigent on the issue of screening players during the auditions, despite the more equitable image such a move would have presented. *The New York Times* of November 18, 1970, reported:

> Earl Madison, cellist, and Arthur Davis, double bass, offered to play man-to-man against any or all of the orchestra's cellists and double bassists, with everyone behind the screens to preserve anonymity. "We have everything to lose," said Mr. Madison. "They have nothing. They say they are the greatest, so let them prove it."

One of the more unfortunate by-products of the Women's Liberation movement is that it can sometimes be used to co-opt the black struggle. For example, institutions like the Philharmonic suddenly adopted a more favorable disposition toward women at the moment when black men were suing them. The women so favored were white, which allowed the positions involved to remain "all in the family," in effect, while a more progressive, liberal image was evoked. Since its inception, the rhetoric of Women's Liberation has tended to fashion itself after that of the black movement. In many instances, one only has to substitute the word *women* for *Blacks*. Largely because of this, the appearance of basic structural changes is given, while in effect the racial status quo is maintained.

This point may be illustrated by the actions of the Philharmonic nine days after the termination of the case against the Philharmonic:

> On November 27, 1970, the New York Philharmonic announced that two women, both white, had been hired as permanent musicians with the Philharmonic. . . . Toby Saks, like Earl Madison, is a cellist. . . . Michele Saxon, like Art Davis, plays double bass.[*]

There are now five white women in the Philharmonic orchestra.

> The women seemed to feel no special empathy for black musicians, and they were opposed to the use of measures such as picketing or petitioning to force the Philharmonic to hire black (or women) musicians.
>
> "I just don't think that an institution that's on the top, like the Philharmonic, should be forced to hire minority group members," Miss Saxon said. "The Philharmonic should have total artistic discretion." Mrs. Benedetti (a cellist) added: "It has to be based on musical ability, it just has to." [†]

The black musician only wishes that it were.

[*] Nat Hentoff, "Un-Chic Racism at the Philharmonic," *The Village Voice*, December 17, 1970, p. 32.
[†] *The New York Times*, April 11, 1971, p. 19.

10

The Need for Afro-American Musical Training Programs

> A lot of white musicians come to me and say: It's all very easy for you to play the drums the way you do, since you and your people have a natural talent for music.
>
> —Mr. J., an anonymous drummer

Despite the old axiom that nothing comes from nothing, there is still a widespread belief that because Afro-Americans are generally adept at the arts of music-making, little or no training is required. The genesis of this bit of spurious logic can be traced to ethnomusicologists who, after discovering the importance of music in African cultures, infer that this is the result of a natural, innate sensibility, rather than an accomplishment requiring hard work!

> Syncopation is the most direct way a musician has of emphasizing weak beats, other than outright accentuation. By transforming his *natural gift* for against-the-beat accentuation into syncopation, the Negro was able to accomplish three things . . .*

Afro-American and African cultures, it is true, place a high value on the arts. But this is an acknowledgment of the humanist aspects of those cultures, rather than an indication of innateness of talent. It simply does not happen that a black child is born with rhythm or, on seeing

* Gunther Schuller, *op. cit.*, p. 16.

a piano or flute for the first time, sits down and immediately produces beautiful music. What does occur is the inculcation of artistic values, into which the child is acculturated, and out of which, if facilities and instruction are available, he gains impetus toward self-expression.

The critics of the idea of a program for the training of black musicians in Afro-American musics argue that Jazz is something that can't be taught, that it is something that one merely has to feel. Of course the "feeling" component must be present, as well as the experiential background of Afro-American culture, but these are not sufficient to produce a level of artistry commensurate with a John Coltrane or a Miles Davis. What is usually mistaken for lack of training is the lack of systematically supported training. However, there exists an entire network of informal training practices, which are to a great extent dependent on agencies outside the Afro-American community. The informal training practices consist of the emulation of musical models from commercially-supported radio and television programs, very few of which involve Afro-American artists; listening to and picking up tips from touring musicians in night clubs, if the young musician is of legal age; and apart from private lessons, which do not include the vital experience of ensemble playing and are extremely expensive, the practice of listening to phonograph recordings.

During the year 1970, *Billboard*, the magazine of the music industry, reported gross income from record sales alone at over $1 billion. Since "classical" record sales have been diminishing, we may infer that the huge returns were due mainly to what has come to be called "rock" music, Blues with another name! This conclusion is borne out by the opinion expressed by the Bank of California:

> By 1975, the rock music recording business will be the fourth largest San Francisco industry, earning gross profits of 150 million dollars per year. This is the opinion of a Bank of California executive expressed in

an article in the March edition of San Francisco magazine.*

Since the mid-Fifties, pseudo-descriptive product labels
of the music industry have undergone rapid change. The
following diagram illustrates this market phenomenon:

1890	1920	1940	1956	1967	1972
Blues	Classic	Rhythm	Rock and	Acid Rock	New
	Blues	and	Roll	Folk Rock	Rock
		Blues		Jazz Rock	
				Country Rock	

Little choice is left for the consumer and aspiring musician since the centralized industry composed of radio,
television and recording companies emphasize to a great
extent the same type of material; that is, whatever has
been contrived by the tastemakers to be the most salable
at that particular time. For example, out of thirteen AM
and fifteen FM stations in the San Francisco Bay Area,
eleven, or close to 40 percent, are rock stations, playing an
average of twenty-five minutes of rock music per half hour.
A sampling of Chicago radio stations reveals a similar
pattern.

There is only one Jazz station in the Bay Area. All of
the disc jockeys are white, except for one who is an Asian
American. Programming, with a few exceptions, leans
heavily on the big-band genre. The Dorsey Brothers, Glenn
Miller or Stan Kenton are more likely to be heard than
"Sonny" Rollins, Horace Silver or Coleman Hawkins.
When national Afro-American groups play the one or
two "big-time" Jazz clubs in the area, there is usually an
increase in the frequency of play given to that artist's
recordings. Once he or they have gone, the station quickly
resumes its previous format. In like fashion, so-called black
stations usually exclude Jazz, air time being given mostly
to other Afro-American musics.

* Joseph Linenmeir, *Musical News* magazine, San Francisco, December, 1970, p. 1.

Television also practices discrimination, in that Afro-American musicians are hired only in token numbers on staff orchestras, and their music is not frequently played —the predominant tendency being toward white rock music and now, in addition, country and western music. What emerges from the above data is an increasing pattern toward the thwarting of the search for self-expression among the creators of Afro-American music. Unlike the symphony and opera, which are in the process of securing systematic support from agencies such as tax-exempt private foundations and the National Endowment for the Arts, Afro-American music is being forced to appeal and develop forms commensurate with the conditioned tastes of the mass audience. Under such conditions, Afro-American musics will find difficulty in maintaining tradition and purposeful artistic direction, but will continue to be fragmented into increasingly mutually exclusive categories. In turn, would-be aspirants to the field are deluged with synthetically produced career models, facilities being unavailable for the type of organic interplay between student and professional musician that is required for the attainment of individualized artistic expression. As a result, in former times, of private and quasi-public support, and at present of foundation and government support, symphony and opera have had no need to change constantly or to become compartmentalized into competing fragments. Contemporary composers such as Aaron Copland and Samuel Barber can continue to write in essentially the same style as in their youth, if they so choose. The entire spectrum of so-called classical music, from Monteverdi to Stockhausen, can be programmed in the mass media without dissent, instead of primary emphasis on the latest "hits."

With systematic support there is reduced need for "polls" which arbitrarily acknowledge some as best and the "greatest this or that," while relegating others to lesser positions on what amounts to an absurd status hierarchy founded and perpetuated by various magazine merchants.

In the field of European classical music, a Stokowski, Casals or Richter is never mentioned as the duke or prince of conductors, cellists or pianists respectively, and rarely as the greatest. Their culture rewards them equally as all being artists and all great once they have achieved a high level of competency. David Riesman's comment is apropos of the stultification produced when artistic models are almost totally dependent on mass media:

> The same forces that consolidate the socialization of tastes also make for more socialized standards of performance. The other-directed child, learning to play the piano, is in daily competition with studio stars. He cannot remember a period when either his peers or their adult guides were not engaged in comparing his performance with these models. Whatever he attempts —an artistic accomplishment, a manner of speaking, . . . the peer group is on hand to identify it in some way and to pass judgement on it with the connoisseurship typical of the mass media audience. . . . Hence it is difficult for the other-directed child to cultivate a highly personal gift. . . . The newer pattern of popularity depends less on ability to play an instrument than on ability to express the proper musical preferences. . . . The need for musical conformity is today much more specialized and demanding than it was in an earlier era, when some children could be, or were forced by their parents to be, musical, and others could leave music alone.*

Recently an eminent scholar remarked that there would have been very few, if any, outstanding Afro-American musicians if equal career opportunities had existed in America. He further stated that music was one of the few careers to which entry was not closed on account of color discrimination. This may seem a persuasive argument if placed in the context of generalized career mobility of various ethnic groups. Certain jobs and trades

* David Riesman, *The Lonely Crowd* (New Haven: Yale University Press, 1956), pp. 76–77.

performed predominantly by a particular ethnic group at one point in time give way, under new conditions, to movements either up or down the ladders of industrial hierarchies. For example, the nineteenth-century building trades in America involved a five-leveled hierarchy made up of English bosses, Swedish supervisors, Irish skilled tradesmen, Afro-American mud tradesmen (e.g., plasterers) and Italian common laborers. After emancipation, the Swedish moved up to the position of bosses, the Irish to supervisors, the Italians to mud trades, and the Afro-Americans down to common laborers. More recently Puerto Ricans and Mexican-Americans have assumed the common labor level, with Afro-Americans again as mud tradesmen, while the Italians assumed the skilled trades, the other positions remaining fairly constant.

However, upon closer inspection the argument breaks down on several levels. The argument assumes that artistic work is conceptually similar to other occupations; in other words, the fundamental importance of music to Afro-American culture is not taken into account, nor is the element of conscious sacrifice and economic uncertainty that thus far marks the career fate of the Afro-American musical artist.

In the same vein, the argument assumes music, and in particular Afro-American music, to be solely the by-product of social forces, discounting its immanent characteristics or reciprocal effects on societal values and change. In terms of the monopolistic structure of the music industry—its channels of production and consumption—the Afro-American has rarely deviated from the role of performer restricted to primary but relatively unprofitable input functions. Only recently have Afro-Americans begun to own recording companies, and even that is on a small scale, compared with companies such as RCA Victor or Columbia, musical conglomerates that place controls over all sectors of the music *and* television industries including promotion, manufacture and distribution. Afro-American

recording "companies" usually turn out to be small independent studios where artists have their recordings taped.
Actual manufacture of the "finished" product and distribution is presently handled by white-dominated syndicates.
(See diagram below.)

Channels of Production and Consumption
in the Music Industry

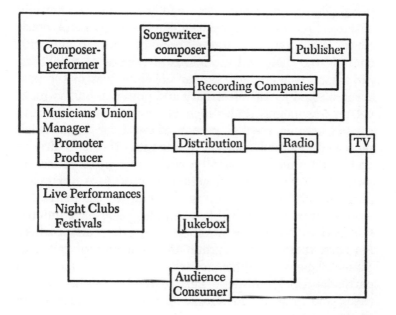

The decline in the number of young Afro-American
players can be partially attributed to an increasing lack
of control over the musical product. As the above diagram
indicates, numerous agencies intervene between creation
of the product and the final output. Furthermore, the
artist may be excised from the market or "covered" by
white imitators at any time, a situation that spells eco-

nomic uncertainty at best.* As the audience becomes increasingly abstract, and further removed from his direct
line of contact, music becomes, as has other modern technology, a matter not of artistic concern and impulse, but
one of the practice of tested formulae guaranteed to satisfy
needs that have been created by the industry. In this way,
Afro-American music has begun to reflect the gadget
orientation typified by so-called rock music. White groups
like the Beatles were able, through electrically powered
instruments, to achieve simulation of the power and emotional intensity that heretofore had been produced entirely
without, or with a minimum of, such aids by black musicians. What white imitators now attempt to do with
controls and dials and thousands of pounds of amplifiers,
pre-amps, speakers, and similar novelties was in the past
accomplished by the electricity and power of *human* mag-
netism. Technology under such circumstances sacrifices the
natural, organic, creative process of music for the artificial,
simulated, canned musical pollutants. If inequality of
opportunity and lack of alternate career possibilities explain the interest in and ascendancy of Afro-Americans
in the musical arts, how do we account for the increasing
number of white middle-class "hippies" who have entered
the field in increasing numbers since the early Sixties?
No barriers attend this group in the matter of range of
career choices or opportunities. Nevertheless music, in
particular "rock" music, seems to hold a fascination for
them, and quite a few sizable fortunes have been made
in this way, despite the appeal to "Lumpen Proletarian-
ism" evinced by blue-denim shirts and funky pants with
American flag patches sewn on their seats.

It seems to this writer that Afro-American musical cul-

---

* *"Covering* is the industry term for the process by which songs recorded by one artist are copied by another. In such cases the black artist
usually loses. Small record labels welcome covers. The reason is simple.
Owning the publication rights to the songs, they make up in song royalties
what they lose in record sales. Songwriters also benefit from covers."
Arnold Shaw, *The World of Soul* (New York: Cowles, 1970), p. 164.

ture offers the only hope of a musical art form in America that is capable of unlimited expansion and growth, provided that significant changes are made in terms of control over outputs as well as input by Afro-Americans in all phases of the music industry related to production and distribution, and in terms of long-range, systematic support from federally financed programs such as the National Endowment for the Arts, for the creation and perpetuation of training institutes for Afro-American musicians on a community, as well as national, level.

It has always seemed an anomaly that European audiences have consistently supported Afro-American music while inexplicable contempt for it has been expressed at home. It is odious that no sustained effort has yet been made to systematically teach Afro-American music and its appreciation in the public schools of America alongside the all too numerous and irrelevant courses in Western European music. Japan, a country over five thousand miles away, does have such school programs.

Beyond the elementary and secondary grades, there are over two hundred college and university programs and eighteen conservatories in the United States that offer professional degrees and certificates for the study of European classical music. Over the past few years there has been a gradual emergence of Jazz programs in colleges and professional schools as well as on the elementary level. The great majority of them are, however, directed by and aimed at the recruitment of white performers. A prominent black musician from the Bay Area recently remarked that a Jazz clinic he taught in 1972 had over five hundred student participants (elementary level), only one of which was black. Moreover, the above programs are often costly and/or located in regions inaccessible to Blacks, particularly those from urban areas. Programmatic texts, often prepared by black musicians, provide white students in these programs with mechanistic, highly rationalized methods for "producing" improvisation and other elements of Afro-American music. On the other hand, few young black musicians are being recruited for the symphonic performance role in similar programs. The reasons given are identical to those in the Arthur Davis case (see Chapter 9).

For many years American public schools have tried in vain to interest white youth (especially males) in the study of the violin, viola and cello. Understandably, in a country now largely peopled by rugged, immigrant stock, the attempt has proved a failure. In such a context, it is generally believed that only a sissy would consider playing an instrument like the violin or viola. And yet for decades the public schools continued to try the impossible. For a while, during and after World War Two, middle-class European string players, often the victims of Naziism, immigrated to America. As a stopgap measure, they were a welcome relief to symphony and opera orchestras. Even so, the pinch was still being felt as far back as 1950. In the past few years there has been a decline in the number of string players arriving from Europe as a result of unstable economic conditions in America and increased prosperity abroad. Meanwhile, the war and postwar generation of immigrant string players has mostly retired.

The string section is to symphony and opera what the rhythm section is to Afro-American music. It is the core, the nucleus, and is fast dying as interest continues to wane. Yet, incongruously, the federal and state governments and "private" tax-exempt foundations continue to pump more and more public and quasi-public monies into these flagging enterprises, while almost totally ignoring the perpetuation and propagation of music created by black people of America.

For fiscal year 1971, Congressional estimates of appropriations for the National Endowment for the Arts and the National Endowment for the Humanities were $40 million. That year $20 million was appropriated for each of the agencies (see Table, pp. 146–148).

Congress then approved $15,090,000 for the National Endowment for the Arts, during fiscal year 1971, with a

$3,500,000 allocation to symphony orchestras, a 244 percent increase over the 1970 appropriation of $1,017,160. This represented over 23 percent of the total National Endowment for the Arts 1971 budget. The allocation for Jazz, the Afro-American classical music, increased from $20,000 in 1970, its first year, to $50,000 in 1971. The 1971 Jazz endowments represented *three-tenths of 1 percent* of the total budget. Note that although a 150 percent increase occurred for Jazz in fiscal year 1971, the net difference comes to only $30,000 as opposed to a 156 percent increase with a net increase of $2,125,000 for the federal-state program. Similar statistical measures are employed in Afro-American college enrollment figures when an increase from three students to nine is termed a 300 percent increase. Beginning with such small bases these impressive statistics are deceptive.

The following tables do not indicate the total expenditures for the year 1970–71, but only include the data which is available to the public. Nevertheless, there are some striking implications even in this incomplete array of statistics. Out of the twenty-nine funded categories, Jazz ranks third from the bottom in terms of appropriations for fiscal year 1971. The highest three categories in terms of funding are the federal-state partnership programs, the symphonies and the professional theater, in that order. The federal government spends seventy-four times more on European-derived symphony music, the orchestras of which blatantly discriminate against Afro-Americans, than on Jazz, which is native to America. A further comparison of these two categories reveals a 150-percent increase for Jazz (but with a net increase of only $30,000) to $50,000, which divided among thirty-one individuals and organizations is an average of $1,600 per grantee.

> Recently the Endowment announced plans for a second round of grants to the art of jazz totalling $50,000. More than double. All together, the Endowment's music program this year is the largest single effort in

1970–1971 National Endowment for the Arts Appropriations (amounts in dollars)

	1970	1971	Percent increase or decrease	Increase or decrease in dollars	Number of grantees	Range of grants	Average grant per organization for 1971
Symphony	1,017,160	3,500,000	244%	2,482,840	73	5,000–500,000	47,941
Opera •	951,000	951,000	00%	0			
Dance •	215,400	330,480	53%	115,080	20	35,000–69,400	16,524
Writers in Developing Colleges	30,000	31,500	5%	1,500	7		4,500
Jazz	20,000	50,000	150%	30,000	31	250–1,000	1,612
Architecture and Design	374,750						
Artists in the Schools	900,000	750,000	–20%†	–150,000†	300+		2,500
Assistance to Arts Organizations	10,538,630						
Assistance to Individual Artists	400,791						
Dance		147,836			16		9,239

• Coordinated residency touring program grants matched by states.
† Minus sign indicates decrease from 1970 to 1971.

1970–1971 National Endowment for the Arts Appropriations (continued)

	1970	1971	Percent increase or decrease	Increase or decrease in dollars	Number of grantees	Range of grants	Average grant per organization for 1971
Visual Arts Intermediate Program		60,000				Varying amounts to 5,000	
Works of Art in Public Places	94,000	100,000	6%	6,000		Varying amounts to 5,000	
Writers in the Schools	164,815	300,000	81%				
Fine Arts in Federal Office Buildings	195,450						
Job Corps (Performing Arts)	75,000						
Chamber Music Concerts	69,550						
Literary Presentations	33,735						
NASA Art Program	5,800						
Indian Arts and Crafts Development	614,000						

1970–1971 National Endowment for the Arts Appropriations (continued)

	1970	1971	Percent increase or decrease	Increase or decrease in dollars	Number of grantees	Range of grants	Average grant per organization for 1971
Artists, Critics, and Photographers in Residence		30,000				1,000– 2,000	
Dance Commissioning/ Production Challenge Grants	153,000	246,700	61%	93,700	1970–2 1971–2	10,000– 150,000	123,350
Federal-State Partner- ship Program	2,000,000	4,125,000	106%	2,125,000	1970–54 1971–55	Max. 1970 36,363; Max. 1971 75,377	75,000
Inner City Mural Pro- gram	9,000	5,000	–80%*	–4,000*			
Museum Program	291,000	1,000,000	244%	709,000	1971–14		71,427
National Endowment for the Arts Treasury Fund	5,627,850						
Professional Experimental Theatre and Workshops (Pilot)	189,000	217,500	15%	28,500	1970–25 1971–22	Up to 20,000	9,886
Professional Theatre (Pilot Program)	1,320,500	1,130,250	–16%*	–190,250*	1970–27 1971–28	5,000– 100,000	40,366
Public Media (Pilot Pro- gram)	195,000					Up to 12,500	
Visual Artists' Fellowships Pilot Program		150,000			20	7,500 per grantee	7,500

* Minus sign indicates decrease from 1970 to 1971.

our five and one half year history. In fact, by the end
of the Fiscal Year 1971, funding for music programming will have come to more than the total obligations
for music during the entire five years of our history.
. . . If music and the other performing arts are to continue without a loss of professional standards, the
federal government must help, state and local government must help, donations from organizations, foundations, corporations, and individuals must help. All of
us concerned with the *value of our culture,* and with
the *quality of our civilization, must help.**

Given the above incongruities in funding, the implications of Miss Hanks's concern over "the value of our
culture" becomes clear. What is meant by *our* culture is
evidently the culture of Europe, not that of America. Inasmuch as Europeans do not pay taxes to the American
government to establish and supply the monies made
available for dispensation by the Endowment, it would
seem that Afro-Americans who do pay such taxes would
be given at least proportionate returns on tax dollars spent.
There were not tens of thousands at Stravinsky's funeral,
as there were in the case of Louis Armstrong.

The Twentieth Century Fund in their 1966 report described the limited audience for the performing arts, and
we can be relatively sure that *performing arts* refers again
to mainly European-derived or European-inspired arts:

> The audience for the arts in the United States is al-
> ready a very limited one. The performing arts attract
> the interest and support of only a minority of the popu-
> lation. The audience at a typical performance is most
> unrepresentative of the general urban population. It is
> dominated by the members of white-collar occupa-
> tions, especially the professions; it is exceedingly well
> educated and very well off financially; . . . Despite
> some tendency toward wider regional distributions,

* Nancy Hanks, "Of Quality in Music," *International Musician,* July,
1971, p. 18.

professional performances are still heavily concentrated along both coasts, and especially New York City.

During the summer of 1971, a sixty-page *Report on Cultural Racism* was compiled by Ishmael Reed, Albert Dennis and the author.* It was distributed to Afro-American artists and public officials. Subsequently, during fiscal year 1972, $60 million was authorized for National Arts and Humanities programs, this time with a primary emphasis on opera. † A new program was established, funded at $1 million, that "will concentrate on the arts of the 'Ghetto' and of 'deprived areas,' rural areas." For fiscal year 1973, $80 million is authorized for arts and humanities programs; at this writing announcements have not been made concerning fiscal 1972 appropriations for Jazz, although there are rumors that the figure will increase fourfold. And although a step in the right direction, it is still far below that required for the performance and training requirements of Jazz musicians. The usual pattern also seems to be forming by which white Jazz musicians and organizations are receiving the bulk of the meager grants.

For those who consider the recent establishment of archives and research centers for Afro-American music at Indiana University or Rutgers to be sufficient, let me say that to establish research and archival centers before establishing training institutions for Afro-American music is like putting the cart before the horse. The main function of these centers is the collection of data and the ordering of materials related to Afro-American music, not the training of Afro-Americans to generate the ongoing activity of musical production and insure its propagation and continuance as live music. Therefore the researcher-scholar

* Ishmael Reed, Albert Dennis, Ortiz Walton, *Ending the Western Established Church of Art, A Report on Cultural Racism* (Berkeley, 1971).

† Donal Henahan, "In Capital, Endowment Unit Will Seek Opera Grant Aid," *The New York Times,* March 16, 1971, p. 46.

at present gains more from archival centers than does the performing artist, whose career and subsequent contribution depend greatly on adequate training facilities. The combination of Afro-American musical training centers and archival centers is, however, another matter. A creative feedback process between the two types of programs might then take place, whereby the student, while undergoing training in all phases of Afro-American music culture, would be in a position to enhance his theoretical knowledge through research. This drawing upon tradition via research facilities would yield greater unity between otherwise disparate categories of the music, a heightened tendency toward performance of all periods and epochs of Afro-American music by contemporary artists, and compositional syntheses which reflect the tradition.

After the Depression and the enactment of a progressive income tax during the presidential term of Franklin D. Roosevelt, wealthy private philanthropists and patrons began to channel their taxable surpluses into large-scale "nonprofit" corporations and foundations. Total taxable income for large corporations could then be reduced by that amount siphoned off into foundation tax "shelters." The revenue slack created by otherwise taxable corporation profits had to be made up by increasing revenues from other sectors, including the private citizenry. To this extent, the existence of foundations is dependent in large part on income and other taxation of the citizenry, amid the growing costs of highly centralized government.

From this standpoint, one may question what share of foundation benefits accrues to Afro-Americans on a general level, and on particular levels like the arts? If there is, as we suspect, little equity between that which is collected and that which is granted, Blacks might benefit more from the lowering or abeyance of such taxation, and the dispersal of these monies directly to Afro-American communities to underwrite cultural and other "welfare" programs:

Government, union and business officials told those at-
tending the thirty-first meeting of Black publishers
held in Atlanta that America must talk about a fair
share of jobs (governmental and foundations appropriations) rather than simple "equal opportunity" practices.*

In addition to grants required for training institutes for
Afro-American musicians, grants are needed for Afro-
American symphonic orchestras such as that headed by
Edward Ellington. His efforts toward perpetuating an
Afro-American aesthetic in music have been legion and
now enjoy a universal appeal which has brought America
international recognition and understanding, serving to
lower the cultural barriers which divide America from
other nations of the world. During 1971, the Ellington
orchestra toured Russia, a nation which has consistently
proclaimed Jazz as decadent. Radio Free Europe Jazz
broadcasts (which, incidentally, are heard in continents
besides Europe) and cultural exchange programs involving Afro-American music, open doors otherwise closed to
American foreign diplomacy. To this extent, the American
government and "private" foundations, which benefit directly from the easing of international tension through
such cultural exchanges and radio programming, owe at
least as much to the maintenance of Afro-American classical traditions as to those of Europe.

One wonders just what exactly is meant by culture on
the level of those whose grants and gifts are aimed so
exclusively at a musical culture which, no matter how
worthy it may be, is nevertheless something other than
that which is only of this nation. I submit that if culture meant American culture, Ellington's music would
be supported in precisely the way the symphonies and
operas are supported and that he would be in residence a month at a time in all our major cities in the
best hall available. In addition, his music would be as
much a part of the standard educational system as the

* The Berkeley *Post*, July 15, 1971, p. 15.

symphony is, as a regular part of each year's curriculum. . . . One of the foundations could do a lot worse with its money than to underwrite a 26 week series by Ellington on National Educational TV. He already has more than enough original works of importance to do it.*

A series by Ellington should, however, include his orchestra as well. For frequently Ellington's solo performances on television are employed as an indication of increased use of Blacks in the media. Such actions fall far short of the ideal as evidenced in a recent statement by Cecil Taylor on Dick Cavett's show:

> The difference between Duke Ellington playing without his orchestra and presenting the totality of his music with those people who have been playing with him for 30 years, and presenting Duke Ellington as a soloist, relegates his effort, therefore, to that of an entertainer because . . . he is not in full control of the musical world that he has created. . . . He is being isolated from the heritage, the condition of the music. †

As the future begins to look increasingly bleak for distinctively American music, it correspondingly looks brighter for symphonies and operas. It becomes obvious that there will never be enough for the latter in terms of governmental and foundation subsidies. As Nancy Hanks has observed:

> It is a basic fact of ironbound economics that the performing arts cannot support themselves. Costs will continue to go up and assistance must rise with them. There is, alas, no way for box office receipts to pay the costs by themselves. That is why the Endowment places such stress on the need for continued and increased cooperation between governments, foundations, corporations, individuals and organizations. ‡

* Ralph J. Gleason, "American Culture and Ellington," San Francisco Chronicle, October 3, 1969, p. 50.
† Cecil Taylor, "The Dick Cavett Show," October 23, 1970.
‡ Nancy Hanks, op. cit., p. 18.

What she doesn't tell us is that one of the reasons for box-office failures, especially in the symphony category which accounts for over 23 percent of the total National Endowment for the Arts budget, is that there are simply too many symphony orchestras to begin with. In New York State alone there are ten major and metropolitan orchestras, five of which are located in the New York City area. There are a total of five major and metropolitan orchestras in both Texas and Ohio.

With modern transportation it is not difficult for European-type orchestras to tour in the same way that Jazz orchestras have been doing for years, even before such facilities existed. In this manner one orchestra could service the symphonic needs of a state or larger area, and cut down on expenses and subsidies for what amounts to a redundancy of effort. This is precisely what occurs with European orchestras *in Europe,* which allows the state to grant more per orchestra since there are fewer to fund. It would seem that few people enjoy hearing the same basic repertory over and over again, even if done by different orchestras and conductors. When the author was a student in New York City, the New York Philharmonic had to give away tickets, since attendance was so poor at concerts. One wonders whether America is trying to out-Europe Europe, with every little town and burg boasting of its own symphony. In Connecticut, for example, there are the Hartford Symphony, New Haven Symphony, Bridgeport Symphony, Stamford Symphony, and probably others that I have never heard of. Young whites have never clamored to attend concerts featuring European symphonic music, and this disinclination has increased with the present "hip" generation, which seems more interested in so-called rock music and the Afro-American music from which it derives.

It means a greater degree of full-time employment for the national and local white performer but less and less for the Afro-American. All one can hope for, if he is an Afro-American who pays taxes like others, is token handouts, unless he happens to have been chosen by Leonard Feather or Leonard Bernstein to be one of the dozen or so "all-stars" who are allowed to make a living playing Jazz.

Nancy Hanks tells of a thank-you letter received by the National Endowment for the Arts:

> "For the past nine months a total of forty-four young aspiring-to-be-drummers/musicians have found, and participated in, a successful search for their musical, and in some cases, personal identity. Every one of them says thank you. . . . The grant was a bulwark against loss of incentive to these possible musician/percussionists of tomorrow. The grant managed to provide a strong alternative to the drugs, television overdose, etc. Thank you for helping to generate a truly Musical Revolution."
>
> It only remains to add that Mr. Reid's grant was for $250.00! In terms of money spent, it was one of our smallest projects. In terms of effect, however, who can say how large it will be.*

Isn't is amazing how resourceful black folks can be with a couple of "bills"! The ole plantation days are here again.

---

* Nancy Hanks, *op. cit.*, p. 21.

11

Toward the Creation of
an Afro-American Musical Industry

> Jazz—it's the American Negro's tradition, it's his music.
> White people don't have a right to play it, it's colored
> folk music. . . . You had your Shakespeare and Marx
> and Einstein and Jesus Christ and Guy Lombardo but
> we came up with *Jazz*, don't forget it, and all the pop
> music in the world today is from that primary cause.
>
> —Charles Mingus, 1971

Even though some sympathetic white writers on Afro-
American music are concerned over the fate and well-
being of Jazz and Jazz musicians, their concern is not so
great as to lead them to suggest that Afro-Americans
control that portion of the music industry which presently
feeds on black talent:

> It is hardly open to question that the black community
> would be far better off were it in a position to control
> one of its leading resources, the talents of its people.
> Under the existing circumstances, however, this is an
> impossibility. Like Peruvian copper or Chilean nitrates,
> the "raw material" of jazz—artistry—is dumped on a
> glutted market where the price it can command is rela-
> tively low; whereas those who dispose of the "finished
> product"—recording companies, festival promoters,
> bookers and agencies, nightclub owners—are, by their
> superior position, enabled to take the "lion's" share of
> the profits.*

* Frank Kofsky, *Black Nationalism and the Revolution in Music* (New
York: Pathfinder Press, 1970), pp. 14–15.

One wonders under what circumstances such an event would be possible. We got no clue from the author. We may only infer from his political orientation that he has in mind a violent revolution, a Communist putsch led by whites but fought primarily by Blacks. Like pie in the sky, it would magically turn over the industry to Blacks if there were any left after the infighting was over. Of course, such arguments, like their counterparts in Christianity, have romantic charm and a millenarian appeal.

It is strange however that Jews and other ethnic groups in America have not gone about establishing and consolidating industries that bring economic and social benefits to their communities in this manner.* Quite the contrary! Other ethnic groups have pooled their invest-

---

* The second wave of Jewish immigration occurred in the middle portion of the nineteenth century and consisted, for the most part, of Jews from various German states. Many of these immigrants arrived relatively impoverished and began their life in the United States as peddlers, fanning out to the communities of the hinterland, the Midwest, the West, and the South to sell their wares. Eventually, the peddler settled down and became a storekeeper and, in some cases, the proprietor of what became the large department store in the large city. . . . Beginning in the 1870's and swelling to substantial proportions in the 1880's and 1890's, the tide of Eastern European Jewry, fleeing persecution and economic dislocation in the lands of the Czars and hard times in the empire of the Hapsburgs, came to America seeking refuge and a new life. Some of these left their ports of debarkation and went to smaller cities and towns as their German predecessors had done. The vast majority, however, because of their poverty, . . . stayed in the larger Eastern cities—and most of these became part of the urban working class in the garment factories. . . . The rise in socio-economic status of the Eastern European Jews and their descendants is, in fact, the greatest collective Horatio Alger story in American immigration history. By the 1940's Jews in the United States had an occupational distribution which showed striking similarities to that of the high-status Protestant denominations. In a national sample studies in 1945–6 . . . 36 percent of the Jews were in "Business and Professional" occupations. . . . In Lenski's Detroit sample of 1957 . . . 43 percent of the Jews were placed in the upper-middle-class bracket. Numerous surveys of Jews in medium-sized communities show them to be bunched overwhelmingly in middle class occupations especially as managers and proprietors in retail and wholesale trade and manufacturing, and increasingly in the professions. [Milton M. Gordon, *Assimilation in American Life* (New York, Oxford University Press, 1964), pp. 183–186.]

ments in those enterprises for which their talents and cultures are best suited, and thus gaining a foothold, have then proceeded to what amounts to a cultural-economic nationalization of their particular resources, buying out or otherwise forcing out competitors, but rarely from an open, violent, street-fighting perspective.

The Afro-American has become heir to the myths that it is better to be poor than rich, lower class rather than middle or upper, easygoing rather than industrous, extravagant rather than thrifty, and athletic rather than academic. Accordingly Afro-Americans, unlike other ethnic groups, are viewed, and often view themselves, as being better off not owning property, business and land. This "capitalism" is good only for Jews, Italians, Poles, Lithuanians, Irish, Germans, WASPS and other ethnic groups residing in America who are in the process of striving to better their lives. It is also good for their middle- to upper-class children, who are called hippies. They indulge frequently in what has come to be known euphemistically as "Mod capitalism," which includes the ownership of large tracts of land, stores of all types, stocks and bonds and even record companies. Regardless of whether the label is capitalism, communism, socialism, or fascism, capital is used and sought by every people and country in the world including The People's Republic of China, which recently criticized the quality of American goods to be used in the trade exchanges established by Richard Nixon.

Wherever one travels in this world, money talks and poverty is silent. Those who doubt this should try going abroad to Africa, China, Russia or Europe without a dime or ruble, and see what happens to them! The critical issue is what is done with the money, or capital, and not its existence in itself.

In a day when black athletes are beginning to invest in capital building enterprises which subsequently employ members of the black community, one looks in amazement at the relative absence of this type of activity among black musicians. Perhaps one of the reasons is that they, like James Brown, will be accused of being black capitalists. James Brown, a highly successful Rhythm and Blues musician, has been a victim of Marxist definitions based upon capitalist exploitation of Blacks by nonblack ethnic groups. Brown's attempts to channel his musical earnings to increase black businesses is nonexploitive, to the extent that they employ Blacks and promote the interests of the black community. The arguments against black ownership based upon profit-making enterprises usually follow the line that not only is profit-making an individual matter inimical to profit-sharing, but that in order to run a business one must first obtain the raw materials or wholesale merchandise from a white capitalist who owns the means of production. A slightly more sophisticated version of this argument is contained in the aforementioned analogy of the music market with the glutted markets for Peruvian copper or Chilean nitrates.

The questions not raised by that author are: 1) Which musicians are responsible for glutting the market? 2) Why is the music market glutted in the first place? 3) Why should not Afro-American musicians and businessmen from the black community, as record company owners, festival promoters, bookers and distributors make use of the raw materials produced by Afro-American musical artistry?

We may infer from the statements of Harold Cruse, and their verification based upon content-analysis samples from radio and television, that it is not Afro-Americans who are glutting the musical market:

> There is only one Sammy Davis. In the shadows, a multitude of lesser colored lights are plugging away, hoping against hope to make the Big Time, for the white culture brokers only permit a few to break through.*

* Harold Cruse, *The Crisis of the Negro Intellectual* (New York: William Morrow, 1967), p. 109.

A sampling of San Francisco Bay Area and national television presentations employing music, over a six-week period, from June 12, 1971 through August 30, 1971, reveals the nature of the glutting, or oversupply.* Seventy-nine percent, or almost four-fifths, of the total number of musical groups presented on TV were white, while one-fifth were Afro-American. Inasmuch as the data were based upon listings in *TV Guide*, and therefore did not include network staff orchestras and symphony orchestras which hire only a token number of Afro-American musicians, the statistics represent only the minimal number of white groups. An even higher percentage would obtain for white groups, if the above inclusions were made in the sample.

Approximately two-thirds of the singles or solo performers listed in *TV Guide* were white. The same proportions obtain for white groups and singles, combined. We may infer from the above data that the glutting of the music market is brought about by the growing proliferation and subsequent promotion and display of white, rather than Afro-American, groups and solo performers. The data also lends strong support to the proposition that Afro-American artists like Sammy Davis are selectively employed as source models for whites to imitate. A characteristic example of the latter, as many Afro-American musicians have observed, was "The Tom Jones Show," on which guest Afro-American artists such as Davis were imitated by Jones during duet performances involving his guest.

Typically, radio stations, excepting those which specialize in news broadcasts or talk shows, feature one classification of music over another. Thus stations come to be identified as rock, classical, Jazz, country and western, Rhythm and Blues or commercial stations, depending upon their predominant content. A cross-sectional survey of AM and FM radio stations and their respective distribution according to the above categories reveals a

* See Appendix.

highly skewed programming in the direction of white rock, country and western, and mixed commercial on AM; FM programming is skewed towards rock, mixed commercial and European classical.

Out of a total sample of seventy-six AM stations across the country, 34 percent were mixed commercial, 24 percent rock, 19 percent country and western, 10 percent Afro-American rhythm and blues and 6 percent each for classical and Jazz. Eighty-four percent of the seventy-six stations surveyed play white music, and 16 percent feature Afro-American music.

From a total of fifty-four FM stations surveyed, 35 percent are European classical, 20 percent white rock, 17 percent mixed commercial, 11 percent country and western, 8 percent Afro-American Rhythm and Blues, and 9 percent Afro-American classical, or Jazz. Eighty-three percent of the FM stations featured Euro-American music and 17 percent featured Afro-American music. (See AM and FM tables.)

Federal Communications Commission (FCC) regulations concerning the licensing of radio and television stations maintain that there should be a distribution of programming responsive to community needs. Inasmuch as the large radio and television stations are operated within the large metropolitan areas, which are becoming increasingly black, some serious questions may be raised. Do Blacks want to hear more Jazz and Afro-Latin music and less rock, commercial, country and western and classical music. To what extent are the Afro-American and nonwhite communities' needs being met, given the previously mentioned statistics?

Questionnaires were distributed in the six cities listed in the cross-sectional survey. Eighty-seven percent of the respondents favored greater programming of Afro-American music on the media. Seventy-four percent felt that present programming should encompass the total historical perspective of Afro-American music, rather than just current fads and novelties.

An experiment recently conducted by Attorney Donald

Warden indicated that members of the white community would also prefer to hear more Afro-American music:

> We once ran an experiment on radio. We played a recording by George Harrison (of the Beatles) called "My Sweet Lord." We played the same tune by an organist-singer, Billy Preston. When we asked the listening audience who they liked, about ninety percent of the Blacks said they liked Billy Preston, and about eighty-five of the whites called to say they liked Preston too. The fact of the matter is, Harrison's tune was No. 1 all over the U.S. and sold millions. Preston's tune did not get off the ground.*

Undoubtedly, one of the major causes for this biased pattern of media programming is the lack of ownership of radio and television stations by Afro-American and other nonwhite ethnic groups.

According to Clifford Alexander, a Washington, D.C., attorney and former chairman of the Equal Employment Opportunity Commission, "Not a single one of the close to 400 commercial TV stations is owned by a Black. . . . Only nine (some say 12) of the close to 2,000 radio stations are owned by Blacks."

Discrimination against black musicians extends beyond radio and television to the biased hiring policies in Broadway and off-Broadway musical productions, Hollywood staff orchestras and musicians' unions. A survey of employment practices in Broadway pit orchestras in New York City, conducted by Robert Magnum of the New York State Division of Human Rights, in 1970, disclosed an almost complete absence of Afro-American musicians in these positions. It would seem to be in the province of the musicians' union to insure equal employment opportunity for all its membership. Equality of employment opportunity has, however, not been the concern of most musicians' unions in the United States.

* Chester Higgins, "Fight Bias in Radio Against Famous Blacks," *Jet* magazine, June 24, 1971, pp. 60–63.

Now that the final mergers have been effected, and the musicians' union is "one big happy family," an economic rather than the previously stated egalitarian rationale is advanced to explain the necessity for mergers (amalgamation) instituted during the past fifteen years:

> We were investigated three times by Congress. Some senators would say to me "you are bragging about a great democratic union—why do you have two locals in many cities and especially here in Washington, D. C.?" And because of this situation we could not put over legislation for the benefit of musicians. Every time President Kenin went to Washington for help, he would get the same story. Not only did Congress go after him, but the President of the United States, through the Secretary of Labor, and George Meany, president of the AFL-CIO.*

We may infer from the above that large national appropriations to discriminatory symphony orchestras is probably a prime example of legislation formerly withheld.

During the same proceedings a resolution (part of which appears below) was offered to establish a fact-finding committee to investigate complaints under the amalgamated system.

> The promises of President Kenin have not been fulfilled and reports from black musicians throughout the country indicate that they have lost job opportunities; been discriminated against; been made victims of tokenism; and been used as "window dressing." All of these situations are directly attributable to the merger of locals and the thrusting of black musicians into the white old line establishment. . . . The Federation Civil Rights Department has never functioned effectively except to encourage or force merger without

---

* James C. Petrillo, "Official Proceedings," from a report adopted by the Seventy-fourth Annual Convention of the American Federation of Musicians, Seattle, Washington, 1972, p. 18. Herman Kenin served as president of the American Federation of Musicians from 1958 to 1970, the period in which the majority of mergers took place.

safeguards to insure the welfare of the minority group.*

Throughout the mid-Fifties and early Sixties, many of the black musicians' union officials often took the politically unpopular position of remaining separate. The arguments for continued separation were of two basic types: those involving territorial prerogatives and those involving monetary assets.

The first argument warned of subsequent loss of jobs by black musicians working within the black community if "amalgamation" materialized. The second predicted a loss of assets, including revenues, buildings, union properties, etc., given that amalgamation by tacit definition would be in one direction only, i.e., black unions relinquishing their franchise and thus integrating into previously all-white locals. Unfortunately both predictions have been borne out by evidence over the past fifteen years.

Let us examine what has occurred in the fifteen-year period between 1955 and 1970. First, from a well-defined homogeneous group, albeit one restricted by social convention to only traditionally allotted forms of music, there has occurred a diffusion of the black musician into a potpourri of white musicians, removing his former professional and organizational identity. Even before the present recession-depression, the black musician worked less, relative to white musicians, than before amalgamation. Furthermore, his opportunities to be engaged in the diversity of musical employment were correspondingly no greater than before.

Assets, in some cases greater than those of the "parent" white local, were transferred to the latter and token formulas worked out to include a minuscule portion of officials from the previously all-black locals. And whereas Black-owned night clubs and cabarets now offered white or mixed bands, white-owned clubs and cabarets persisted in hiring mostly all-white groups.

* Otis Ducker, *Ibid.* See Resolution No. 10, p. 10.

Petitions and informal meetings between semiorganized black musician groups and Local 6 San Francisco officials (an example that may be generalized nationally) have not produced egalitarian results: There is still a noticeable absence of Blacks playing boat or cruise jobs or appearing with the San Francisco Symphony ballet or opera.

Consequently, black musicians vis-à-vis amalgamation-integration are no longer recognized as a special-interest group, in the manner of rock or symphony musicians, and are not assisted in expanding or diversifying their talents in remuneratively profitable musical enterprises, such as Frank Zappa's and J. Maggioni's rock-symphony concerts. In other words, Afro-American musicians within white-dominated "amalgamated" unions have become amorphous and are losing their identity as a group.

An interesting departure from the amalgamation syndrome is the union of the late Charles (Charlie) Parker. Local 627, Kansas City, Missouri, was one of the last to remain separate despite the Federation's decree that all of its unions amalgamate. President Richard Smith explained why, after heavy pressure from the power structure, his local has chosen to remain separate:

> We have a certain definite culture. I think that it has been recognized all over the world. The jazz as such stems from the African beat . . . and has been brought over here. . . . We feel we are an individual group, an ethnic organization capable of planning our own future. We feel we have shown through the years that we can stand alone. We can stand separate and not have to ask anyone for favors nor expect any generosities. We have gone along in this organization, and we feel it has made a definite contribution to Kansas City Music and music in general. We do not feel that we owe anyone an explanation as to just exactly what we stand for.
>
> We have been here as an organization since 1918. There have been quite a number of things that have tended to more or less force us into a situation and we know there is no success formula to it. We know that

mergers as such, and we have seen this over the years, have proven that there is no material worth to the Black Man—to the Black Musician. As you know, I am interested in music more than anything else. I do not know what mergers have done in other fields, but I do know what they have done in the American Federation of Musicians. *

Conditions are getting no better for Afro-American musicians; according to most accounts they are getting steadily worse. Jazz, the Afro-American classic, is becoming a universal, something which everyone may use or profit from, even before compensatory rewards are allotted the sources of the music, the Afro-American musicians. Until they gain a degree of broad organizational consensus and build supportive institutional structures, control over music and products will remain in the hands of others.

An essential step toward the creation of an Afro-American music industry concerns the involvement of Afro-American communities. The economic thrusts now taking place in black communities have rarely taken into account resources that have already been developed—the arts, and in particular the music arts. The ownership of recording companies and communications media goes hand in hand with the engagement of Afro-American Jazz musicians in live performances. Such performances are the quintessence of the art and provide the means by which tradition is maintained and the vital social functions of Jazz are activated.

* Earl X (Franklin) and Clarence 3X (Kenner), "Union of Charlie Parker, K C Local Union Chooses Not to Integrate with White Group," *Muhammad Speaks,* February 13, 1970.

Recorded Examples of African Vocalization and Instruments

Musical Concert or Instrument	Tribe-Country	Record Company & Catalogue No.	Name of Recording	Title of Selection	Name(s) Performer If Given
vocal glissando	Kouyou (Congo Republic)	Ducretet Tomson D2F1S4	"Anthologie De La Vie Africaine"	"Complaint of the Sinners"	Solo voice
wide vocal range and speed of execution	"	D2F1S4	"	"Therapeutic Chant"	
work song	Vili (Congo Rep.)	D1F1S23	"	"Preparing Meal"	
vocal antiphony	Kouyou (Congo Rep.)	D3F1S8	"	"Historical Story Teller"	
talking drum gong	Fang (Gabon)	D2F1S1	"	"Talking Drum Gong"	
talking xylophone (marimba)	Fang (Gabon)	D21S1	"	"Talking Xylophone"	
conversation between xylophone and dancers					
earth bow	Ba-Bembe (Congo Rep.)	D1F1S10	"	"Earth Bow and Voice"	
antelope trumpet	Kouyou (Congo Rep.)	D1F2S7	"	Antelope Horn Trumpet	
talking drums and earth bow	West Africa	DL8446	"Africa Speaks, America Answers"	"Chant"	Guy Warren
miriton: hollow bone with spider-web covering—forerunner of Kazzo	Baegbo Ivory Coast Mali Guinea	UNESCO BM30L2301	The Music of the Dan	"The Mask"	
the Trumpet Orchestra—6 ivory (elephant) trumpets using Hocket technique	Dan (Guinea Mali)	"	"	"The Trumpet Orchestra"	
work song (sound of grinding is used as accompaniment)	Senufo—Ivory Coast Guinea, Mali	BM30L2308	"The Music of the Senufo"	"Song of Woman Grinding Millet"	

Appendix

Name of Black Source	*Name of White Performers (Imitators)*
Louis Armstrong	Everything and Everybody up to 1941
Johnny Dodds	Benny Goodman
Barney Bigard	Artie Shaw Woody Herman
Johnnie Hodges	Willie Smith, Franki Trumbauer
Lester Young	Stan Getz, Zoot Sims, Al Cohn, Brew Moore, Bill Perkins
Charlie Parker	Everybody Lee Konitz, Art Pepper, Phil Woods, Charlie Mariano
Bud Powell	Bill Evans, Al Haig, Everybody
Fats Waller	Jess Stacey, Art Hodes
Miles Davis	Chet Baker, Shorty Rogers, Jack Sheldon
Jimmy Blanton	Bob Haggart
Oscar Pettiford	Chubby Jackson
Jimmy Harrison w/Basie Ellington	Red Mitchell Bill Harris Tommy Dorsey
J. J. Johnson	Urbie Green Carl Fontana Frank Rosolino & Everybody

Sonny Rollins   Sal Nistico
Dexter Gordon   Pepper Adams
Sonny Stitt   Joe Barrel
John Coltrane   Everybody
Stuff Smith   John Lee Ponty
                                 Joe Venutie
Sid Catlett   Gene Krupa
  and Chick Webb   David Tough
                                 Louis Bellson
Max Roach   Buddy Rich
                                 Shelly Manne
Charles Mingus and James   Scott LaFaro
Blanton   Steve Swallow
                                 David Inzenson
                                 Charles Haden
Billie Holiday   Peggy Lee
                                 Lee Wiley
Ella Fitzgerald   Chris Conncrs
                                 Dinah Shore
                                 June Christy
                                 Anita O'Day
Buddy Bolden, Scott Jop-   Original Dixieland Jazz Band and
  lin, Jelly Roll Morton   Dixieland
Fletcher Henderson *   Everybody and Everything Swing
  Don Redman, J.
  Lunceford, Count Basie
Lester Young, Miles Davis   West Coast School
Charlie Parker,
  Thelonius Monk
  Dizzy Gillespie
John Coltrane   Avant-Garde
Cecil Taylor
  Ornette Coleman

* Wrote Benny Goodman's most popular arrangements.

A Sampling of Proportion of Black and White Performance on Television

White Groups	Black Groups	Combined Total
45	12	57

White Singles	Black Singles	
53	26	79

Combined Total = 98   Combined Total = 38   136

Percentage of White Groups = 79
Percentage of Black Groups = 21

Percentage of White Singles = 68
Percentage of Black Singles = 32

Percentage of White Groups and Singles Combined = 72
Percentage of Black Groups and Singles Combined = 28

Item Analysis of Readers Guide *Inventory of Musical Articles Published Between the Years 1919–1970, Based upon Subject Listings* *

Subject Listings of Euro-American Music	Number of Articles
American Opera	390
Analysis	185
Appreciation	211
Boston Symphony	43
Festivals	54
History and Criticism	236
Instruction and Study	259
Music (Classical, symphonic, etc.)	398
Music U.S.A. " "	377
Musicians " " "	324
Operas (reviews etc.)	521
Orchestras	288
Single Works	38
Theory	3
	3,327

* Percentage of total is 86%.
* Between the years 1919–1949, the figures represent the total number of articles in these categories with references in the *Readers Guide* for each year during this period, for the Fifties through Sixties a three-year sample was used, and for 1970 a one-year sample was taken.

Subject Listings of Afro-American Music	*Number of Articles*
Jazz	356
Negro Music	37
Negro Musicians	29
Negro Songs	64
	486

* Percentage of total is 14%.

Cross-Sectional Radio Survey: Programming Emphases, AM

	Jazz	Rock	Country and Western	Mixed Commercial	Afro-American Rhythm and Blues	Classical European	Total Stations
New York	1	3	2	6	1	1	14
Chicago	2	2	1	4	3	1	13
San Francisco Bay Area	0	5	2	3	1	2	13
Great Falls, Montana	0	4	2	1	0	0	7
Los Angeles	2	2	3	10	2	1	30
Fayetteville, North Carolina	0	2	4	2	1	0	9
Totals	5	18	14	26	8	5	86
Percent of Total	6%	24%	19%	34%	10%	6%	

Cross-Sectional Radio Survey: Programming Emphases, FM

	Jazz	Rock	Country and Western	Mixed Commercial	Afro-American Rhythm and Blues	Classical European	Total Stations
New York	1	3	0	0	2	6	12
Chicago	1	1	1	2	0	3	8
San Francisco Bay Area	1	6	1	4	0	3	15
Great Falls, Montana	0	1	0	0	0	0	1
Fayetteville, North Carolina	0	0	1	1	0	0	2
Los Angeles	2	0	3	2	2	7	16
Totals	5	11	6	9	4	19	54
Percent of Total	9%	20%	11%	17%	8%	35%	

Index